James A. Simpson is a native of Scotland. It was in Glasgow that he had his primary, secondary and tertiary education. At Glasgow University he studied maths and nuclear physics. He later studied divinity at the same university, gaining a scholarship to study for a year in New York. After ministering in Falkirk and Glasgow he moved in 1976 to Dornoch in the North of Scotland to become minister of the town's mediaeval cathedral. During his 21 years there he wrote several books including *Holy Wit*, which for many weeks topped the Scottish bestseller charts. Dr Simpson is a regular contributor to magazines and newspapers, not only in Scotland, but also in Ireland and the USA.

In 1992 he was appointed a chaplain to the Queen in Scotland. Two years later he was elected to the office of Moderator of the General Assembly of the Church of Scotland. In 1995 he was awarded an honorary doctorate by Aberdeen University.

D0854891

BY THE SAME AUTHOR

There Is a Time to...
Marriage Questions Today
Doubts Are Not Enough
Keywords of Faith
Holy Wit
The Master Mind
More Holy Wit
All About Christmas
The Laugh Shall Be First
Life, Love and Laughter
A Funny Way of Being Serious

Laughter Lines

Family Wit and Wisdom

James A. Simpson

Steve Savage
LONDON AND EDINBURGH

Steve Savage Publishers Ltd
The Old Truman Brewery
91 Brick Lane
LONDON
E1 6QL

www.savagepublishers.com

This revised edition published by Steve Savage Publishers Ltd 2007

First published in Great Britain by Gordon Wright Publishing Ltd 1987

Copyright © Rev James Simpson 1987, 2007

ISBN 978-1-904246-28-2

Typeset by Steve Savage Publishers Ltd
Printed and bound by The Cromwell Press Ltd

Copyright leased to the publisher. No part of this publication may
be reproduced, stored in a retrieval system, or transmitted, in any form,
or by any means, electronic, mechanical, photocopying, recording or
otherwise, without prior permission of the publisher.

Contents

To Helen With Love

'Laughter is the sun that drives winter
from the human face'
Victor Hugo

'You cannot understand the most serious things in life
unless you understand the most humorous'
Winston Churchill

Introduction

Laughter was part of my childhood. I was fortunate in being born into a happy fun-loving home, for humour is a saving grace. It preserves sanity in times of stress. It can relieve irritation and tension. It can prevent family arguments getting out of hand and family disputes becoming broken homes.

Our country is being hard hit today by the breakdown of family life. There are many reasons. One seldom mentioned is that many families have forgotten how to laugh together. What infuriating creatures we can all be. Humour helps us not to take ourselves too seriously. The ability to laugh at our own shortcomings and idiosyncrasies is a mark of maturity.

Kindly fun and humour bring greater stability and vitality to family life. When we joke and laugh together, we stop being just husbands and wives, parents and children, and become good friends who enjoy being together. My father's lively sense of humour certainly enriched my early years.

After-dinner speakers soon discover that once humorous anecdotes or witty remarks are spoken or written, they become public property. There is no copyright in the field of humour. While many of the stories in this book are true, others are obviously apocryphal. But they all have this in common – they made me smile or laugh when I first heard them.

I hope that like my other books, this small volume of family wit and wisdom will also produce a few chuckles. I have written it because I believe family life would be enriched if we took fun and humour more seriously.

The royalties from this book will be donated to help finance further research into cystic fibrosis, a crippling disease which afflicts many lovely children, including my own granddaughter.

James A. Simpson
"Dornoch"
Bankfoot
Perthshire

Not Even a Number

A little girl was explaining to her friend the age of her new baby brother. 'He is so little he's not even a number yet!'

Muriel Thomson, one of Britain's leading women profess-ional golfers, was the middle member of female triplets. The week after they were born, her father, who was a keen golfer, was greeted at the club with cries of 'One under fours again', and 'I see you are still three putting.'

A church congregation sat enthralled while a young, very pregnant woman rose in the choir and sang, 'O Lord make haste and deliver me.'

A mother tells how the day their first child was born, her husband was ecstatic. His concern for her was really tender. Five years later, after the birth of their fourth son, he was considerably more casual. He walked into the hospital after work, slumped into a chair, and exclaimed, 'Whew. What a day I've had!'

A young sailor asked if he could have leave of absence for the birth of his child. His commanding officer smiled and said, 'I know you were necessary nine months ago for the laying of the keel, but are you really needed for the launching?'

Two expectant mothers on their way to the ante-natal clinic were overheard discussing doctors in general. Finally one said, 'At least in our case, they can't say, "It's all in the mind".'

A woman confined to hospital with high blood pressure was anxiously awaiting the birth of her first child. Believing that some flowers might boost her morale, her mother phoned the florist and asked him to deliver a bunch of roses with a card bearing the message, 'Hoping this will improve your morale. Love, Mum.' The flowers, when they arrived at the hospital, caused considerable embarrassment, for the card was addressed to Miss rather than Mrs, and it read, 'Hoping this will improve your morals.'

Tension reigned in the operating theatre during a particularly difficult birth. Later, when the crisis was past and the baby had been taken away to be weighed and bathed, the anaesthetist asked the obstetrician whether it had been a boy or a girl. 'I honestly don't know,' said the obstetrician. A student nurse who was standing nearby said coyly, 'If you let me see the baby, I could tell.'

An army sergeant tells how among the numerous forms he had to complete when signing on in the army, was one containing the question: 'Number of children (by sex)'. One answer was: 'Two, and one by adoption.'

The only time a woman wishes she was a year older is when she is expecting a baby.

There is only one thing for which a man is never fully prepared – TWINS.

In the life of many houses there are two periods – BC and AD. Before Child and After Disturbance.

Anyone who sleeps like a baby hasn't got one.

Infant care has to be learned from the bottom up.

Training a baby is always a matter of pot-luck.

To correspond with the Biblical text inscribed over the door of the old Sick Children's Hospital in Glasgow, one wit suggested that over the door of the new adjacent Maternity Hospital, they should inscribe another text. 'We shall not all sleep, but we shall all be changed.'

The young father was rewarded with a first-time smile from his baby son. Awe-struck by this first smile, he turned to his wife and exclaimed, 'Darling, he's friendly.'

When little Margaret returned from Sunday school she asked her father when their new baby would talk. He told her that it would probably not be for two years, since little babies don't talk. 'But they did in the Bible', said Margaret. 'The teacher told us this morning that Job cursed the day he was born.'

The distinguished Spanish singer Teresa Berganza once sang in the Milan Opera House when she was pregnant. She later said of the performance, 'I had much less stage fright with the baby in me, because I thought of him and not the audience. He was quiet when I was singing, but as soon as I stopped, he started to applaud with his feet.'

A proud mother once remarked to Churchill that her baby looked exactly like him. 'Madam', he replied, 'all babies look like me.'

Dr James Hall tells of once receiving a phone call at 3am. One of his patients was having labour pains. Since she was not due for two weeks, he told the husband to phone back when the pains were twenty minutes apart. Three hours later the husband phoned again. His wife didn't think she could wait until the pains were twenty minutes apart. When Dr Hall asked how far apart they were now, the husband replied, 'They've been five minutes apart ever since I rang you up the first time.' They just made it to the hospital in time.

When a lady inquired of the Inland Revenue if birth control pills were deductible for tax purposes, she was told, 'Only if they don't work.'

A Liverpool lady whose husband works with the Post Office tells how her husband phoned the maternity hospital to see if the baby had arrived. The ward sister informed him he had a lovely little boy. Not knowing that he was a postman, she was understandably puzzled when he asked her to tell his wife he would be in to see her after the second delivery.

Earlier this century many wives were worn out with childbearing. I think of the wife of a Scottish grocer who had borne twenty-four children. Like the previous twenty-three, the twenty-fourth was born at home. As the doctor filled in the form for the registrar, he turned to the father and inquiring about the date, asked, 'Is this the 26th?' Thinking the doctor was inquiring about the size of his family, the father replied, 'Oh no, doctor. It's only the twenty-fourth.'

Madame Aubernon, the French woman of letters, tells of how the young son of two of her closest friends one day asked his father, 'Papa, when you and Mama went on your honeymoon, where was I?' The father hesitated just for a moment, and then said, 'Son, you went there with me, and came back with your mother.'

Babies are such a nice way to start people.

Angels or Devils

'Children,' said one grandfather, 'are those little angels that arrive on Monday and those little devils that leave on Saturday.'

Ralph Erickson tells of a statistician who promised to look after his four small energetic children while his wife went shopping one Saturday afternoon. When she returned, he gave her a note that read: 'Dried tears – 11 times. Tied shoe-laces – 15 times. Blew up toy balloons – 5 per child. Average life of each balloon 10 seconds. Warned children not to run across the street – 26 times. Number of Saturdays I will go through this again – Nil.'

A father tells how his son came home from school looking rather nervous. 'Dad, I have a message for you. There is going to be a small meeting of the Parent-Teacher Association at school tomorrow.' 'What do you mean by "a small meeting"?' asked his father. 'Well,' said the lad, 'It's just you, me and the headmaster.'

Another boy came home with a dreadful report card. As his Dad read it, the colour drained from his face. But before his father could say anything, the boy said, 'Dad, I was wondering. Do you think it's heredity or environment?'

A mother, puzzled by the teacher's remark that her child was 'adept in the creative use of visual aids', finally discovered it really meant, 'copies from the child next to her.'

Martha Herman, who had received a toy watch on her fourth birthday, asked her father to put it on her wrist just like his watch. Her father proceeded to place the watch on Martha's left arm. Standing facing him she saw that his watch was on the other side. 'I want my watch on the same arm as yours,' she said. 'That's what I'm doing,' replied her father. 'I wear my watch on my left arm, and I'm putting yours on your left arm.' But Martha didn't understand left from right. She just knew her Daddy was putting her watch on the arm opposite his. He tried to explain that when she turned around, her left arm and his would be on the same side. But she couldn't grasp that. With tears running down her cheeks, Martha said to her father, 'Did God make me wrong?'

Mary was four years old. Her mother took her to the first of her dancing classes. The room was filled with wee boys and girls trying to learn the difference between left and right feet, trying to stand on one foot and falling down, turning and bumping into one another. As they were driving home after the first lesson, her mother asked Mary how she had liked her dancing teacher. 'She was all right,' said Mary, 'but she never told us when our first show would be.'

A little boy rushed in from his swimming lesson to announce that he had jumped from the diving board. 'But you told me that last week,' said his mother. 'I know', he answered sheepishly, 'but last week I was pushed.'

> The smile of a child as he starts for school,
> Is a bit restrained as a general rule.
> The teacher's smile, in the same way tends
> To droop a bit as the holiday ends.
> But the smile much wider than the others,
> As the summer riot ends, is Mother's.

15

A wise infant teacher sent the following note to the parents at the start of the school year. 'If you promise not to believe everything your children say happens at school, I will promise not to believe everything they say happens at home.'

There is, however, another side to this. Children seldom misquote us. They usually repeat word for word what we should not have said.

How come kids who walk home together have to use the phone to say 'goodbye'?

One person, more honest than most said, 'I grew up to be the kind of child my mother would not have wanted me to play with.'

A mother was baking pancakes. Her two boys James and Ryan were arguing over who was to get the first pancake. The mother saw an opportunity for a moral lesson: 'If Jesus was sitting here, he would say, "Let my brother have the pancake. I can wait."' There followed a pause, before James turned to his younger brother. 'Ryan, you be Jesus.'

The following advert appeared in a local newspaper. 'A loving kitten desires position as companion to a small child. Will do light *mouse* work.'

After minor medical treatment to his arm, the nurse asked the little boy if he wanted a bandage. 'Yes,' he said, 'but could you bandage my good arm.' When the nurse asked why, pointing out that bandaging the sore arm could prevent infection and let his friends know not to touch it, the wee lad said, 'You don't know my friends.'

🐾

Parents of the 33rd Paisley Scout Troop were rather worried when they received a note from the Scout leader. Part of it read, 'Last year the subscriptions were, Cubs £10. Scouts £12. From this figure, £5.50 is sent for each boy to Scout Headquarters as the decapitation fee.' One parent pointed out that although she was happy to be rid of her son for one night a week, she felt 'decapitation' was going too far.

🐾

It was a wise school-master who said to the parents, 'I cannot control your child in the High School, if you haven't controlled him in the High Chair.'

🐾

One father said, 'My son is at an awkward age – too young to spell establishment, but old enough to defy it.'

🐾

A father and mother were upset by their daughter's limited vocabulary. Everything was either 'amazing', or 'ghastly'. They sometimes heard these two words more than fifty times a day, depending on whether their daughter liked or disliked something. Finally, the father said, 'Mandy dear, there are two words your Mum and I don't want to hear any more. One is ghastly and the other is amazing.' 'OK Dad,' Mandy answered agreeably, 'What are they?'

🐾

A child coming out of the music examination said to her Mum, 'I think the examiner must be a very religious man. He kept putting his head in his hands and saying, "Oh my God".'

🐾

A boy who had said some very cruel and nasty things to his younger brother refused to apologise. His mother tried to appeal to his better nature, but with little success. Just before bedtime she tried a different approach. 'Look James, how would you feel if your wee brother died tonight? I'm sure you would feel terrible about having said these awful things to him, and not having said sorry.' This seemed to win the day, for she heard him go through to his brother's bedroom and say, 'I'm sorry,' but then he added, 'But if you are not dead in the morning, I'll thump you.'

Little Jimmy desperately wanted a BMX bike, but his parents said they could not afford it. That night he prayed, 'Dear Jesus if you give me a BMX bike, I promise to be good for three months.' But then he had second thoughts. Three months was a long time, so he prayed, 'Sorry Jesus, I made a mistake. If you give me the bike, I will be good for a week.' But again he thought, a week is a long time. Then he had a brainwave. Going over to his bedroom mantelpiece, he removed the little statue of Mary that was there. He then took it and locked it in one of the drawers. Then getting back on to his knees, he prayed, 'Dear Jesus, if you don't give me the BMX bike, you will never see your mother again.'

A man spent a whole afternoon cementing holes in the pavement in front of his house only to have a seven-year-old come along on his bike and make ruts in the fresh concrete. The man yelled at the boy, using some blistering words. Hearing the man's language, the boy's mother said, 'He didn't mean it, and anyway, I thought you loved children?' 'I do,' said the man. 'But in the abstract – not the concrete.'

Children are very adept at comprehending modern statistics. When they say, 'Everyone else is allowed to,' it is usually based on a survey of one, or perhaps two.

When a four-year-old was asked what he was going to be when he grew up, he gave the inquirer a scornful look and said, 'Bigger.'

A Yorkshireman tells how their son was learning to play the clarinet at school. Progress was painfully slow. In practice he produced some excruciating sounds. Eventually he was banished to the garden when practising. At first the neighbours were most understanding, but one day one leant over the garden wall and said, 'Hello son. What are you going to be *if* we let you grow up?'

A Glasgow mother took her two children to Loch Katrine. There she showed them the two great pipes that brought the water down from the loch to the City of Glasgow. When one of them inquired why there were two pipes the older one, who knew all the answers, said, 'Don't be silly. One is for the hot water and the other for the cold.'

We all need recognition, but one little boy carried it a bit far. 'Dad, let's play darts. I'll throw and you say, "Wonderful!"'

The present generation is the first to be raised by three parents, the third being the television set in the corner of the room. This was highlighted by one child's answer to the question, 'What does this century owe to Edison?' 'If it was not for Edison,' she said, 'we would all be watching television by candlelight.'

Growing Pains

A teacher tells how he spent two weeks explaining Dante's *Divine Comedy* to his class of fourteen-year-olds. He kept stressing that the poem was an allegory of the poet's journey through hell, heaven and purgatory. When he came to mark their exam papers, he found one boy had described the poem as a journey through 'hell, heaven and puberty'. What a freudian slip!

You realise your children are growing up when:
A box of sticking plaster lasts longer than a week.
'Mummy, Mummy, becomes 'Hey Mum.'
When you find the free gift at the bottom of the cereal packet.
When you can't help them with their homework any more.
When the car they want for their birthday isn't from a toy shop
When they stop asking for money and request a loan.

To a youth who had just made some dogmatic statement, an old village philosopher said gently, 'When I was your age, I knew far more than I do now.'

It never seems to occur to adolescents that one day they will be as dumb as their parents.

The great secret of dealing successfully with an adolescent is not to be his or her parent.

Father Bernard Vaughan travelled one day in a train with a young man who greatly irritated the other passengers with his language and appalling manners. At last the young man got out. As he passed the carriage window, Father Vaughan knocked on it and shouted, 'You've left something behind.' The young man dashed back, frantically mouthing, 'What?' As the train began to move, Father Vaughan shouted through the window, 'You've left a very bad impression.'

A mother tells how her husband, herself and their teenage children were holidaying in Germany. Often during the holiday, the staff in hotels and restaurants would laugh when her husband spoke to them. On one such occasion one of the boys said sarcastically, 'Dad's definitely a lot funnier in German than in English.'

Peering above, probing beneath
Curling her lashes, brushing her teeth
Daubing her face with every new mixture
The teenage daughter's a bathroom fixture.

A teenager once said to his father who was reading a newspaper, 'I know you are listening to me Dad. Your knuckles are white.'

A vicar tells how as a bachelor he preached a sermon entitled 'Rules for raising children'. After he got married and had children he revised the sermon title to 'Suggestions for raising children'. When his children got to be teenagers, he stopped preaching on that subject altogether.

❧

The all too common attitude of teenagers to their parents is summed up perfectly in two remarks – that of a teenager to his friend, 'My Mum wants me to take a trip round the world, but I want to go somewhere else,' and that of a boy buying a shirt. 'Do you mind if I bring it back if my mother likes it?'

❧

A mother who was discussing with a friend the latest problems she was having with her teenage daughter, said sadly, 'We named her Helen Joy. And you know, it has been that ever since.'

❧

The notice advertising the talk at the women's meeting read, 'Is Premature Greyness Hereditary?' One passer-by was heard to comment, 'Yes, I got mine from my kids.'

❧

A lad who had been learning to type asked his father one night if he was going to be using his typewriter. When his Dad said that unfortunately he was, the boy said, 'You won't be needing the car then, will you?'

❧

An astounded teenager answering the phone said, 'Of all the crazy things. It's for you, Dad.'

❧

The only thing that teenagers wear out quicker than shoes are parents.

There are many books for parents on understanding adolescents. What we need is a book for adolescents on understanding parents.

Teenagers today have so many luxuries in their own bedrooms – computer, television, mobile phone and iPod – that the most effective way to punish them is to send them to your room instead of theirs.

A young man was being discussed by two young ladies. 'He is so tender,' said the one. 'Perhaps,' said the other, 'that is because he has been in so much hot water.'

Emblazoned on the T-shirt of a teenager were the words 'Nobody knows the trouble I've been.'

The closest to perfection adolescents ever get, is when they fill out a job application form.

Somebody remarked about the Hit Parade, 'If that is what the top twenty are like, I shudder to think what the bottom twenty are like.'

A young man who was asked what books had most influenced his life, suggested two. 'My mother's cook book and my father's cheque book.'

A. A. Joyce, the distinguished headmaster of an Approved School, once said to the boys at a school assembly, 'I wish you would remember that it is not my school, it is ours. If you spoil the lawns, you are not spoiling my lawns, they are ours. If you run away and do wrong, you damage not only your reputation or mine, you damage ours.' He went on to emphasise the fact that life cannot be lived selfishly, in terms of yours or mine, but must always be lived on the basis of ours.

At the end of the Assembly, one boy came up to him. 'That was a good talk sir.' he said. 'I have been thinking about what you said, and I wondered if you would give me one of our cigarettes?' Mr Joyce smiled and said, 'Certainly, if you will give me some of our money.'

A twelve-year-old boy was watching a Western on TV. His mother was known for her strong convictions about drink and swearing. She came into the room just as the 'hero' was on his way into the saloon. The lad said, 'Don't worry Mum. He's not going to swear or drink. He's only going to kill a man.'

A young boy was constantly asking to be driven places. After his third request one day, his mother said, 'What do you think God gave you two legs for?' The reply came quickly: 'One for the accelerator and the other for the brake.'

The Romantic Years

In Spring a young man's fancy turns to thoughts of love –
and in Summer, and in Autumn and in Winter.

🍂

A young woman's heart, like the moon, is always changing.
But there is always a man in it.

🍂

When Johnny and Mary started dating regularly, both sets
of parents became alarmed. Mary's parents informed her
that she could not marry Johnny unless he became a Roman
Catholic. So she went to work on him, talking to him on
every date about her church, giving him literature to read.
At last she got him to agree to attend instruction classes. All
seemed to be going her way until one Saturday night when
Mary's parents returned home they found her crying
uncontrollably. When they inquired what was wrong, she
said, through her sobbing, 'We have overdone it. Now
Johnny wants to become a priest'

🍂

A young Taiwanese man wrote some 700 love letters to his
girl friend in the years 1974–76 trying to persuade her to
marry him. His persistence finally brought results. The
United Press reported that the girl had become engaged –
to the postman who had faithfully delivered all the letters!

🍂

The Rev David Maclennan tells of an incident which
brought smiles to the faces of a Canadian congregation. The
once-famous professional hockey player Andy Blair was
'going steady' with one of the sopranos in the local church
choir. One evening when he was present in church, she sang
the popular gospel song, *In the Garden*. There was

considerable mirth as she sang the refrain: 'Andy walks with me. Andy talks with me, Andy tells me I am his own.'

❦

When John told his friend that the girl he had been dating had rejected his proposal of marriage, his friend smiled and said brightly, 'Don't let that get you down. A woman's No often means Yes.' But this brought little comfort. 'The trouble is', said John, 'she didn't say "No". She said "Phooey".'

❦

When a father informed his wife that he thought his daughter's boyfriend had been there long enough, and that he really felt he should go downstairs and say good night to him, his wife urged caution. 'Don't forget how we were when we were young.' 'That does it', said her husband. 'Out he goes!'

❦

Earlier this century a John McKinlay courted and finally married one of Scotland's finest woman athletes. When asked how he had managed to catch a girl who could run so fast, he replied, 'She ran towards me.'

❦

When a courting couple kiss, they get so close they cannot see anything wrong with each other.

❦

'Daddy,' shouted Jean from the top of the stairs, 'I'm going for a shower. If Billy phones, tell him to phone back at 7pm. If John phones and Billy doesn't, tell John to phone at 7pm, but if they both call, tell John to call at 7.15pm. If Jimmy calls and Billy and John don't, tell Jimmy to call at 7pm, but if they both call (Billy and John) or one calls, tell Jimmy to call at 7.30pm.'

❦

A Taiwan mother kept disapproving of the girls her son courted. A friend finally suggested that he should find a girl who was like his mother. Several months later, the young man informed his friend that he had found a girl who looked, talked and behaved very much like his mother. 'Good,' said his friend. 'No,' said the young man, 'This time my father disapproved.'

A lady tells how when she first met her husband, he was a patient in the ward where she was an Air Force nurse. She had gone into his room to administer an injection. Now when people ask her husband how he managed to trap and marry an officer and a nurse, he smiles and says, 'She needled me into it.'

'When you are courting you lie a lot,' said a new bride. 'I said I couldn't cook and my fiancé said he couldn't care less.'

A young man tells how in a moment of extravagance he promised his girlfriend a gold watch for her Christmas. When the assistant in the jeweller's shop told him the price of the one he liked, he let out a low whistle in amazement. Pointing to another tray he asked how much they were. 'To you sir,' replied the assistant, 'about three whistles.'

A similar story tells of a young couple looking for an engagement ring. Pointing to one in the display cabinet, the assistant reached for the key to open the case. 'Oh never mind,' the young man said. 'If you have to lock it up, I can't afford it.'

Thomas Beecham's sister had a friend called Utica Welles. Once when they were out walking, Beecham said to her, 'I don't like your Christian name. I'd like to change it.' 'You can't,' the girl replied, 'but you can change my surname.' And so they were married.

The Tangle of the Aisle

A wedding is a ceremony at which a woman takes a man for what he is, or what he has.

Minister to bride at the wedding service. 'Do you Jean ... let me finish ... Do you Jean take this ... Please let me finish, Jean.'

When the minister asked the perspiring bridegroom, 'Do you take this woman to be your wedded wife, for better or worse, for richer or poorer, in sickness...' the bride finally interrupted: 'Please sir, you are going to talk him right out of it.'

At the rehearsal for his daughter's wedding, Otis Skinner, the famous American actor, asked the minister what he was supposed to say in reply to the question, 'Who giveth this woman?' 'You don't say a thing,' replied the minister. 'You just hand your daughter over.' 'Nonsense,' said Skinner, 'I have never played a walk-on part in my life.'

With dieting so commonplace nowadays, would it be wise to add 'through thick and thin' to the marriage vows?

Two friends were arguing about the forthcoming marriage of a colleague in his late 60s to a young lady in her late 20s. 'I don't believe in these May–December weddings. After all, December is going to find in May the freshness and beauty of springtime, but whatever is May going to find in December?' The other replied, 'Perhaps Christmas.'

'Mum,' said the bride-to-be, 'my wedding has to be perfect. We must not overlook the most insignificant detail.' 'Don't worry dear,' said her mother, 'he'll turn up.'

An usher at a wedding, after seating a large group of guests, saw a very attractive older woman enter the church. 'Are you a friend of the bride?' he inquired. 'Good heavens, no,' she whispered. 'I'm the mother of the groom.'

Some ministers get tongue-tied at weddings. One clergyman meant to say 'You are now lawfully joined', but said instead, 'joyfully loined.'

In a Church of England service the nervous father of the bride once responded to the vicar's question 'Who gives this woman...?' with, 'Her father and I do.'

An aristocratic lady said to her newly engaged daughter's fiancé, 'You should have come and asked me before you proposed to my daughter.' 'Should I?' he replied. 'I had no idea you yourself were so keen on me.'

Several ten-year-olds were one day overheard fantasising about a wedding. The one playing the minister said, 'Will you take this woman to be your *awful* wedded wife?'

Dr Nelson Gray tells of a Glasgow wedding he conducted. The groom, as often happens, was very anxious. Things went fine until after the signing of the legal document. Suddenly he gave an anguished yelp. 'Here minister. What arm does Jean take?' It had dawned on him that there was a protocol for newly married couples leaving the church and that he did not know it. Neither in fact did Dr Gray. But then all of a sudden Dr Gray remembered one of those sentimental wedding traditions. 'I told him that the bride always leaves the church leaning on the arm nearest her husband's heart.' But this information proved of little help. 'Jings Mr Gray!' he pleaded in a panic-stricken whisper. 'What one's that...?' There was worse to come: 'My heart's in my mouth.'

What a furore there would be if people had to pay the minister as much for marrying them as they have to pay a lawyer to get a divorce.

The Rev J. Inglis tells of once marrying two very thin young people. The bride's family had nicknamed them 'String' and 'Bean'. After the wedding, nobody threw rice or confetti – they threw *green beans*.

A bridal couple were discussing their approaching marriage. 'I'm not having any of this Woman's Lib stuff, the lad declared firmly. 'I'm going to be boss and you'll do as I say.' Then he added, 'Is that all right with you?'

When a shrewd businessman was asked for his daughter's hand in marriage, he offered a quantity discount to the young man if he would take his wife as well.

An elderly Chinese lady once gave her views on picking a husband. She said she was glad her parents had picked her husband for her. Baffled by this, one western lady asked, 'Why?' 'Well', she said, 'I would hate to think I picked him myself.'

Have you noticed how people seldom think alike until it comes to buying wedding presents?

To Have and to Hold

Marriage is the only union that can't be organised. Both sides think they are management.

An American Rabbi received a thank-you note from a bridegroom he had married. 'Dear Rabbi, I want to thank you for the beautiful way you brought my happiness to a conclusion.'

While interviewing a man for a job, the lady director of the company asked how he would feel about having a woman boss. He hesitated, then smiled and said, 'Well, I suppose I'd feel at home.'

The most serious impediment to marriage these days is the difficulty of supporting a wife and the government on one income.

Nowadays women don't hire domestic help. They marry it.

A cynical husband is reported to have said to his son who was doing English homework 'Marriage is neither a verb nor a noun. It's a sentence.'

Before marriage a man catches a woman in his arms. After marriage he catches her in his pockets.

Before marriage a man declares he will be master in his own home or he will know the reason why. After marriage he knows the reason why.

Before marriage when a man holds a girl's hand it is love. After marriage it's often self-defence!

Part of the problem today is that many couples are well prepared for the wedding, but not for the marriage.

In marriage, being the right person is as important as finding the right person.

The honeymoon is over when he phones that he'll be late for dinner, and she has already left a note that it's in the refrigerator!

A man never used to know a woman had any old clothes until he married her.

'For centuries wives have been misjudged and mistreated,' thundered an exasperated wife. 'They have suffered in a thousand ways. Is there any way that women have not suffered?' 'Yes,' said a quiet masculine voice. 'They have never suffered in silence.'

A Mr Sutcliffe tells how for long it was a source of irritation to him that his wife always had the last word in every argument about his shortcomings. On one such occasion he thought he had triumphed when he said: 'Look here, I would remind you that you took me for better or for worse.' 'I know I did,' she replied. 'But you are worse than I took you for.'

32

To prove his love for his wife one man swam the swollen river, crossed the barren desert and climbed the highest mountain. She divorced him, however, because he was never at home.

Three kinds of men have difficulty understanding women – young men, middle-aged men and old men.

A professor was once asked about the milestones in his life. 'There were three,' he said, 'The day I got a First at Cambridge, the day I became a professor, and the day my first book was published.' 'What about the day you were married?' asked his friend. 'I thought,' he replied, 'you asked me about the milestones, not the millstones.'

Marriage teaches us self-restraint, forbearance, and a lot of other qualities we would not need nearly so badly if we had stayed single.

A farmer, watching a bride and groom emerging from the church, was overheard to say to his son, 'Ach, it's just like the Budget ... you hope for the best but prepare for the worst.'

Max Kauffman said, 'I never knew what real happiness was until I got married. And by then it was too late.'

George Ade said, 'If it were not for the presents, an elopement would be preferable.'

Fortunately there are higher views of marriage.

Something every couple should save for their old age is their marriage.

Agatha Christie, who was married to an archaeologist, once said, 'An archaeologist is the best husband a woman can have. The older she gets, the more interesting her husband finds her.'

One of the truest and loveliest things ever said about marriage was said by Humpty Dumpty. 'I'll never ask advice about growing old', said Alice. 'Too proud?' the other inquired. Alice felt indignant at this suggestion. 'I mean,' she said, 'that one cannot help growing old.' 'One can't perhaps,' said Humpty Dumpty, 'but two can.'

During a discussion on public speaking, one wife confessed that the finest after-dinner speech she ever heard consisted of just four words. 'I'll wash up dear.'

The American writer Erma Bombeck said that the personal possession that had given her the most value for money was her wedding ring. 'For years it has done its job. It has led me not into temptation. It has reminded my husband numerous times at parties that it is time to go home. It has been a source of relief to a dinner companion. It has been a status symbol in the maternity ward. It has reminded me every day of the last thirty years that I have someone who loves me.

On the occasion of their golden wedding a couple shared with others the secret of their happy marriage. The husband said, 'I have tried never to be selfish. After all, there is no "I" in marriage!' The wife said, 'For my part, I have never corrected my husband's spelling.'

Many a wife has found that hugging her husband is the best way to get round him.

A film star said, 'It is easy to make twenty men fall in love with you in a year – but to make one man love you for twenty years, that is real achievement.'

An American lady tells of a very capable black woman who was for some time her domestic help. The black woman's husband was a happy-go-lucky fellow. Though very likeable, he never seemed able to keep a job, and seldom bothered to try. One day when she was asked why she put up with him, she replied, 'It's like this. I makes de livin' and he makes de livin' worthwhile.'

On the occasion of his retirement from Riverside Church, Dr Harry Fosdick said he had been puzzled all his life by the fact that, on the whole, women have not accomplished as much in a public way as men have. Obviously, he said, the brains of women are as good and perhaps better than the brains of men. Yet the sober truth is that there have been relatively few women on the list of outstanding composers, artists, theologians, scientists and statesmen. 'At last,' said Dr Fosdick, 'I know the answer. No woman ever had a wife.'

André Maurois once suggested that the following vow be made part of every marriage ceremony: 'I bind myself for life! I have chosen; from now on my aim will be, not to search for someone who may please me, but to please the one I have chosen.'

The Rev Dr David Read tells how when he applied for American citizenship, he was sent a very complicated form to complete. One of the questions surprised him. 'Have you committed adultery since coming to the United States?' A British friend who had previously been through this procedure, told him he had phoned the authorities about this question. 'Is it really necessary?' he inquired.

George Thomas, the former Speaker of the House of Commons, was given the honour of reading the lesson at the Royal Wedding of Charles and Diana. The passage chosen was that magnificent definition of love in Paul's letter to the Corinthians: 'Love is patient; love is kind and envies no one. Love is never boastful or conceited or rude...' Several months later he told a friend how he had received letters from all comers of the world wondering if he could send them a copy of the wonderful speech he had made at the Royal Wedding.

A successful marriage demands a divorce; a divorce from your own self-interest.

For Better or Worse

Someone once said, 'You find your heaven or hell in the one you marry.'

Lloyds of London will insure almost everything except the success of a marriage.

Most weddings are happy. It's trying to live together afterwards that causes all the problems.

One evening Willie looked up from his homework and said, 'Mummy, how do wars begin?' 'Well dear, the First World War began because Germany overran Belgium.' On hearing this her husband looked up from his newspaper and said, 'It didn't begin that way at all!' Upset at being contradicted, his wife said, 'Willie did not ask you.' 'Well for goodness sake tell him the facts and not the fairy tales,' retorted her husband. And so it went on, husband and wife becoming more and more angry, until finally, Willie interrupted and said, 'It's all right, I think I know now how wars begin.'

A husband and wife could not agree. They had many quarrels. One evening in a reflective mood the husband said, 'I don't see how we cannot agree more often. Look at the cat and dog lying there before the fire in perfect peace.' 'Aye,' said the wife, 'but tie their tails together and see what will happen.'

Notice on Marriage Counsellor's door. 'Back in an hour. Don't Fight.'

The problem with mixed marriages is not that he is Protestant and she is Roman Catholic, or that he is British and she is Japanese. The problem is that he is a man and she is a woman. That is the mix of it.

🐝

'My husband,' said one wife, 'is a nuisance I can't do without.'

🐝

In one sense everybody marries for 'love'. If what a person loves most is money, or position, or security, or looks, or pleasure-seeking, then this is the love the marriage is based on.

🐝

It has been said that a little incompatibility in marriage is the spice of life – provided the man has the income and the wife is pattable.

🐝

It never ceases to amaze me how marriage is often an alliance of two people:

> One who never remembers birthdays, and one who never forgets them.
> One who cannot sleep with the window shut, and one who likes it open
> One who is scrupulously tidy, and one who is untidy.
> One who squeezes the toothpaste, and one who rolls it.
> One who refuses to believe there is a leak in the water or gas pipe, and one who is convinced they are about to asphyxiate or drown.
> One who wants to go home early from a party, and one who wants to be the last to leave.

🐝

Some people in winter are prone to freeze,
While others sweat and smother,
And by some tricky quirk of fate
They marry one another.

🐝

In this connection it is comforting to remember that Jack Spratt and his wife did not have exactly the same likings in the matter of meat, yet history does not record that they were an unhappy couple.

Many a woman has won her husband's love in her best dress to lose it in her worst.

During an interview on the subject of Woman's Lib., an American woman said, 'I'm happy. I like being my husband's slave. I can manage him better that way!'

Marriage is made in heaven. So is thunder and lightning.

The French actress Micheline Presle suggested as proof of woman's superiority over man – 'Have you ever known a woman who married an idiot just because he had beautiful legs?'

A wife is reported to have said to her husband, 'All right, I will admit I was wrong if you will admit I was right.' Such 'compromise' reminds me of the couple who were redecorating their bedroom. The wife wanted to paint it white, the husband blue – so they compromised and painted it white.

When a man complained to his friend that his wife always had the last word, the friend replied, 'Count yourself lucky. Mine never gets to it.' Another said, 'All wives have the last word – some in arguments, others in clothes.'

A father tells how when his son who had just passed his driving test came home and reported a slight accident to their new car, his wife screamed at him, 'I told you to go with him the first time he drove alone.'

A timid little man approached a policeman on the street corner. 'Excuse me officer, but I have been waiting for my wife for over an hour. Would you be good enough to order me to move on.'

Discussing Britain in the 1980s, a domineering wife said to her husband, 'Do you realise that the two most powerful people in Britain today are women, Margaret Thatcher and the Queen?' 'As far as I am concerned,' her husband said, 'the three most powerful people in this country are women.'

'I never try to tell a story', said one husband. 'My wife has an *interferiority* complex.'

A rather self-satisfied author who was glancing through a copy of his new book which had just arrived from the publisher, finally put it down, gave a contented sigh and stared into the fire. A few seconds later he said, 'I wonder how many really great men there are in the world?' 'I don't know dear,' said his wife, 'but I know there is one less than you think.'

Anybody who does not know that a woman's work is never done, isn't listening.

Husbands are also far from being paragons of virtue.

'Before marriage a man declares that he would lay down his life to serve you,' said one wife, 'but after marriage he won't even lay down his newspaper to talk to you.'

A poster advertising a 'Body-Building Course' contained the statement, 'Strong, well-built men often make placid husbands.' The comment of one observer was, 'I am not so sure about that, but I know some strong well-built women who have made placid husbands.'

A cartoon highlighted the common complaint of wives that their husbands 'never tell them anything'. The cartoon depicted a couple who were together one night at home. The television had broken down. The wife turns to knitting, the husband to reading. Then the wife says, 'I think you might talk to me while I knit.' And the husband replies, 'Why don't you just knit to me while I read?'

When I asked the Rev Henry Duncan of Pinehurst if his wife also played golf, he replied, 'Oh no. There has to be one good listener.'

A husband is a man who, after emptying an ash-tray, manages to look as if he had just finished cleaning the house.

A man advertised in the paper for a wife. 'I am fifty-eight years old. Would like to marry a woman of thirty who has a tractor. Please send picture of tractor.' We all know the type.

A wife tells how one night when life was weighing heavily on her husband's shoulders, she left him watching the late night news and went to bed. Hoping to cheer him up, she left a little note on the dressing table. 'Cheer up, things could be worse. You could have my job!' The next morning she found a note pencilled at the foot of her note, 'No, thanks. I couldn't stand your husband.'

&

A husband returning from work one day, found the house in complete chaos. 'What's happened?' he asked his wife. She replied, 'You know how you are always wondering what I do all day? Well here it is. I didn't do it.'

&

'The worst thing about a dispute,' said a wise wife, 'is that it spoils a discussion.'

&

On one occasion Socrates' wife scolded him and then dumped a bucket of water over his head. He did not react as most men might have. Being a true philosopher, he is said to have remarked that after so much thunder and lightning, a shower was to be expected.

&

A paragraph in the *Evening Standard* reported the comment of a Judge in a Divorce Court. 'Though your wife threw several domestic utensils at you, she was not being cruel, for on almost every occasion she missed.'

&

The judge addressing the couple standing before him said, 'Why don't you settle the dispute out of court?' 'Sure that is what we were doing, my Lord, until the police came and interfered.'

&

An elderly man, married for almost forty-five years, returned home one afternoon to find his wife packing. 'What are you doing?' he asked. 'I can't stand it any more,' she cried. 'All these years of fighting, arguing, bickering. I'm leaving.' The husband stood there for a moment bewildered, watching her struggle through the door with her packed suitcase. He then ran into the bedroom and snatched up another suitcase. 'Wait a minute,' he cried. 'I can't stand it any more either. I'm coming with you.'

🐿

Angry wife to husband. 'You are being deliberately calm.'

🐿

Woman on scales to husband. 'That's inflation for you. What used to be 130lbs is now up to 150lbs.'

🐿

Husband to wife. 'I'll tell you whether I still love you when I find out what you are leading up to.'

🐿

When a man brings flowers home to his wife for no reason, there usually is a reason.

🐿

The secret of a happy marriage is that each partner should be willing to give way 51% of the time. Another secret is choosing the right parents!

🐿

On the occasion of their golden wedding a husband was asked to what he attributed his good looks and ruddy complexion. 'Well,' he said, 'It's like this. Before my wife and I got married, we resolved that if ever we were going to quarrel, I would put on my cap and go for a walk. And man, I have lived a grand open-air life.'

🐿

Report in local paper: 'The couple were married on Friday, thus ending a friendship which began in their schooldays.'

🐿

The Belfast police stopped a car at two in the morning and asked where the driver was going in such a hurry. 'I'm on my way to a lecture,' he replied. Suspicious of the answer,

43

the police inquired where the lecture was being held. The driver gave an address identical to the one on his driving licence. 'And who will be giving this lecture?' inquired the constable. 'My wife,' replied the man sadly.

The ultimate in satire was when a wife said to her husband at breakfast, 'I'm fed up with your sour face. Why don't you prop up a newspaper in front of it like other husbands do?'

Eileen Sneddon, a member of my Glasgow congregation, recalls how when she was expecting her first baby, her husband insisted that he would see himself out in the morning. One evening they had quarrelled, and she had gone off to bed in the huff. The following morning he woke her up and said, 'Eileen, we were silly to quarrel like that last night. Come on down and have breakfast with me. I've got it all ready.' There in the kitchen was the most glorious ham and egg breakfast. On finishing it, she happened to glance at the clock, to discover it was twenty-five minutes past midnight! Her husband Robert, determined not to 'let the sun go down on their anger', determined not to go through the night without speaking, had just waited until one minute past midnight before wakening her up. At the time, she could have choked him, but now looks back on the incident as one of the most cherished moments of their marriage.

A puritanical old lady had become totally captivated by the BBC series *The Six Wives of Henry VIII*, one programme being devoted to telling the story of each wife. When this very fine series came to an end, she was overheard saying to a friend, 'For the first time in my life I am sorry Henry had only six wives.'

44

One-Eyed Parents

Mothers

A mother ought to have one blind eye and one deaf ear, but only one.

A child wrote, 'Mummies are for telling you to ask Daddy. Daddies are for telling you to ask Mummy.'

The role of today's mother is to deliver her children obstetrically once, and by car forever after.

Mother no's best!

A child wrote, 'Mummies are for telling you to ask Daddy. Daddies are for telling you to ask Mummy.'

Another said, 'A Mummy is someone who sends you to bed when you are wide awake and wakens you up when you are fast asleep.'

It is important that mothers with small children save something for a rainy day – patience.

A sweater is a garment worn by a child when his mother feels chilly.

Automation is a technological process that does all the work while you just sit there. When we were younger, this was called 'Mother.'

There is a lovely story about a Supermum who was perfection itself. She did everything right – kept a perfect home; kept her husband happy. Always had a copy of the Bishop's latest book on the coffee table – and answered the door pregnant when the priest came by. One day she was asked how she did it. She replied, 'I emulate the Blessed Virgin Mary.' The lady who asked the question said, 'Marge it's a little late for that.' 'Very well, I'll tell you,' she said. 'Every evening when the children are bathed and tucked up in their clean beds, and the lunches are lined up and the shoes cleaned, and I've heard all their prayers, I fall down on my knees and say, "Thank you God for not letting me kill one of them today".'

A lady, filling in a form in a paediatrician's office, tells how beside the blank marked 'Occupation' were these words: 'If you devote the greater part of your time to loving, caring and making a home for your family, put a big star in this space.'

A few mothers get up bright and early. Most just get up early.

Heredity is what a mother believes in, until her child begins to behave like a delinquent.

Mothers often long for the day when their children are out of nappies and at school. Later you hear them say, 'They don't remain babies nearly long enough.'

Somebody has pointed out that of the sixty-nine kings of France, only three were really loved by their subjects. These three were the ones reared by their mothers instead of tutors or guardians. Whatever ability most of us have to make others love us, is largely due to the love our mothers put in and around our lives. Though many factors shape the personalities of our children, the three most essential are love, discipline and independence.

🦋

Fathers

Most people go through a transition in their assessment of their father.

4 years: My Daddy can do everything.
14 years: Dad does not understand. He is hopelessly old fashioned.
24 years: He comes up with a good idea now and then.
34 years: I must find out what Dad thinks about it.
54 years: I wish I could talk it over with Dad.

🦋

It is admirable for a man to take his son fishing, but even more admirable for him to take his daughter shopping.

🦋

A mother tells how when she and her five children went out one Sunday, her husband looked forward to a quiet afternoon watching television and reading the Sunday papers. When they returned they found a sign on the front door: 'Tim is not at home. Deborah is not at home. Kevin is not at home. Sean is not at home. Brian is not at home. There is only a grouchy old father at home.'

🦋

A father told a parent-teacher's meeting, 'We need some old-fashioned honesty in this school. I bring home pencils from the office where I am employed for my kids to use, and within a few days, some other kid has swiped them.'

🦋

A father complained that when he was a boy he had to hide his smoking from his parents. 'Now,' he said, 'I have to hide it from my children.'

❧

When a teacher asked her class, 'Do you think people can predict the future with cards?' one little boy responded, 'My mother can. She took one look at my report card and told me what would happen when my father got home.'

❧

A harassed father confessed to a friend, 'I've felt like running away from home more often since I have had children than when I was a boy.'

❧

A survey finds that the most frequent statements by fathers to their children are:

> 'I'm too tired.'
> 'We don't have enough money.'
> 'Keep quiet.'

❧

One little lad said, 'Dad always used to say, "We'll see." I soon learned that what he really meant was "No".'

❧

Sam Levenson had a similar complaint. 'When I was a boy my father was the boss. Now I am a man, my son is the boss. When does it get to be my turn?'

❧

The most important thing a father can do for his children is go on loving their mother.

❧

'Integrity and wisdom are the keys to business success,' said a father to his son. 'By integrity, I mean that when you promise a delivery of merchandise on a certain day, you must do so even if it bankrupts you.' 'And what is wisdom?' asked the son. 'Don't make such promises.'

❧

'When I was younger,' admitted one father, 'I used to camp with my boys. We ate the fish we caught on our canoe trips. We slept on blankets on the hard ground at night. Now my idea of roughing it is to turn the electric blanket down low.'

❧

Dr Spock and Professor Dewey, two world famous 'experts' on bringing up children, said many wise things, but both I believe understressed the importance of being firm with children as well as being kind to them. One cold winter's day, Professor Dewey was out walking with his little boy. The youngster who was wearing sandals, having refused to wear anything else, was seen splashing around in a large puddle. A neighbour who was passing said, 'If you don't get that child out of the water he will catch pneumonia.' 'I know that,' said Professor Dewey. 'I'm simply trying to find a way of making him want to come out.'

❧

It was different with Harry Fosdick's father. In his autobiography, Dr Fosdick tells how as his father was starting for work one morning, he turned to his mother and said, 'Tell Harry he can cut the grass if he feels like it.' Then after a few steps, he turned back and added, 'Tell Harry he had better feel like it.'

❧

A mother remembers the time when her daughter moved into a flat and she was worried sick about her living alone. The result was she often took her out in the evening to the theatre or to dinner or visiting. Each time she dropped her off at her flat, her farewell remark was 'Now be good.'

Finally her daughter replied, 'Look Mum. You are here almost every night. When do I have a chance to be bad?'

🦋

Wise parental advice:

In bringing up children, spend on them half as much money and twice as much time. To bring up a child in the way he should go, travel that way yourself once in a while.

🦋

The good parent is simply one who more than half the time does and says the right thing rather than the wrong thing.

🦋

Teach your child good manners. They are like the zero in arithmetic; they may not be much in themselves, but they are capable of adding a great deal to the value of everything.

🦋

Bismarck once said, 'You can do anything with your children if you play with them.'

🦋

Good character, like good soup, is made at home.

🦋

Every mother is a working mother.

🦋

A Canadian author Solange Rolland tells how whenever her father, who was a connoisseur of literature, went out of the house, he had a curious way of saying, 'I have hidden the key to my bookcase under the clock in the living room. Please do not read my books.' By the time Solange was fifteen, she had read most of her father's favourite authors.

🦋

A young man tells how once on a railway journey, when his father unintentionally did something silly, he was unmercifully bawled out by a minor train employee. When the lad later asked his father why he did not give the chap a piece of his mind, his father smiled and said, 'If a man like that can stand himself all his life, surely I can stand him for five minutes.'

❦

A Dr Luccock writes, 'One way to be a bad parent is not to get any fun out of the job. We live in antiseptic and homogenised days and nights, when for every sterilised bottle in the refrigerator, there is a book of baby lore on the shelf. Many parents are so weighed down by the responsibility of keeping Junior on schedule to the split second, and keeping his little soul from being scarred with frustration, that they become philosophers with worried looks instead of amateurs having the time of their lives.'

❦

A former neighbour had her house burgled twice while on holiday abroad. On her return she asked my wife what we did with our precious things when we went on holiday. 'Oh,' said Helen, 'we take the children with us.'

❦

It's good to have money and the things money can buy, but it's also good to check up every so often to make sure we haven't lost the things that money can't buy.

❦

If credit cards were called more accurately 'debit cards', would so many people use them?

❦

I grudge not the wealthy whose riches are envied
I wish them prosperity, favour and more
But give me the cottage where little feet prattle
Where love pours the coffee and meets you at the door.

The Afternoon Snoozers

'A grandmother,' said one little girl, 'is that old lady who sits in the corner of the room and keeps your mother from hitting you.' Another said, 'My gran is a knitting machine. She knits all the time, even though we have socks for at least the next five years.'

❧

One little boy wrote, 'Grandparents are old on the outside, but young on the inside.'

❧

One grandfather complained that by the time the youngest children have learned to keep the house tidy, the grandchildren are on hand to tear it to pieces again.

❧

Grandpa who was eighty-eight had little use for doctors. His eyesight was, however, failing quite markedly. His children and grandchildren put pressure on him to go and see a specialist. Finally he agreed. When the smiling doctor asked him what brought him, he replied, 'Interfering relatives.'

❧

Michael Crawford, the actor, had a unique relationship with his grandmother. Though eccentric in some ways, she was a lovely person. He recalls how one night she came to see him in *Billy Liar*. At one point in the play he used a four-lettered word. His grandmother, who was in the box nearest the stage, rose and shouted out, 'Michael, you must not use that kind of language. You were not brought up that way.'

On another occasion, when his grandmother was present in the theatre, towards the end of the play, he turned to the leading lady, and on bended knee said to her, 'Did I do good?' Again to the amusement of everybody in the theatre, his grandmother shouted out, 'You did wonderfully Michael.'

When a tiny three-year-old referred to her Sunday School as 'Sunny School', her 'impartial' grandfather said he was sure her presence would help make it that.

The good news about grandchildren is that they keep you young. The bad news is that after you spend time with them, you feel your age.

Grandma Moses was the grand old lady of the 20th-century art world. She did not begin her whole new career as an artist until she was in her late seventies. Anny Mary Moses described herself as a primitive artist. She was a farmer's wife who painted country scenes remembered from her childhood. She became a celebrity and went on painting till her death at the age of a hundred and one!

An American Baptist preacher Jerome Engel was once annoyed by an old gentleman who fell asleep during his sermon on several Sundays. To the man's grandson who regularly attended with him, the Rev Engel said, 'If you will keep your grandfather awake during the sermon, I will give you a dime every week.' For the following two weeks, the old man listened attentively. But the third week he dropped off again. Sending for the boy, the minister said, 'Didn't you agree to keep your grandfather awake for a dime?' 'Yes sir', the boy replied, 'but now Grandpa gives me a quarter not to disturb him.'

❧

Dr Ernest Campbell tells of a man who longed to have a grandchild. The man's three daughters and their husbands were visiting. When they sat down at the table the father intimated that he had something to tell the family. 'Your mother and I miss the patter of tiny feet about the house, and we have talked it over. I made a lot of money this year and we have decided to give 10,000 dollars to the first grandchild in the family.' Then he bowed his head to say grace. When he finally finished, only his wife and himself were at the table.

❧

Early last century, a little boy was sent one cold winter's day to get some ice-cream from the café. Friends were coming for dinner that night. His mother gave him a large glass jug. The custom then was for so many scoops of ice-cream to be put in the jug. On the way home he saw some of his pals playing football. Joining them for a few minutes, he placed the jug with the ice-cream in it on the wall. As ill-luck would have it, the ball hit the jug. It fell to the ground and smashed into a thousand pieces, the ice-cream splashing everywhere. He was naturally in an awful state, scared to return home. Finally one of his pals said, 'Johnny, have you not got a granny you could go to?'

❧

If you are over the hill, why don't you at least admire the view?

A grandfather with serious hearing problems finally accepted his doctor's suggestion to get a hearing aid. On his return visit to the surgery he thanked the doctor for encouraging him to have an aid fitted. 'My hearing is ever so much better.' When the doctor said that his family must be really pleased, the man replied that he had not told them about the vast improvement in his hearing. 'I just sit around and listen to the conversations I used to miss. In the light of what I have heard, I have changed my will three times.'

Like most grandfathers I am incurably biased. Once while out walking with my one-year-old granddaughter Sally, a dear old lady approached me. Having observed the joy on my face, she said, 'I see Mr Simpson that you have gone back to family worship!'

Grandmother lived with her family. She was active and enjoyed going out each Thursday afternoon to play bridge with her friends whom she referred to as 'the girls'. One day her little granddaughter was in the front yard when her friends drove up to collect her. The little girl ran into the house crying, 'Grandma, the girls with the grandma faces are here.'

Thoroughly Embarrassed

A woman with a small child boarded a one-man bus and dropped a single coin into the box. The driver stopped her. 'That child is older than five, madam. You'll have to pay half-fare for him.' The woman bristled. 'But how could he be older than five? I've only been married four years.' 'Madam,' said the driver, very politely, 'I'm taking fares, not confessions.'

Dr Morris, the minister of Glasgow Cathedral, was formerly chaplain to Peterhead Prison. He tells how his wife sometimes came out to the prison in the car and waited to give him a run home. On one occasion, she was sitting with her son in the car. David at that time was about five. A couple of prisoners' wives and their offspring arrived and waited for the gate to be opened to admit them for their visit. One of these children, catching sight of David, said, 'My Dad's in there.' To which David replied with pride and innocence, 'So is mine.'

The Rev Oscar Johnson tells how, after a change of churches, he met at a party an attractive woman who had been a member of his former congregation. 'How do you like your new minister?' he asked. Her response produced a few wry smiles. 'Oh he's fine,' she said, 'but he doesn't hold me the way you did.'

On one occasion, when on holiday with friends in the Mull of Kintyre, I was asked to open the Carradale Sale of Work. At that time we had three children, and my wife was visibly expecting our fourth. Our friends Tom and Moira also had three young children. To give them a night out on their own, my wife took their three boys with our own three to the Sale. The following morning, when Moira went to the baker's to collect the morning rolls, she overheard one customer discussing with the shopkeeper the previous evening's Sale, and the minister who had opened it. Somewhat disapprovingly she said, 'You know he has got six young children, and he has got his wife in the family way again.' Moira chuckled inwardly, but to her great shame, never confessed that three of them were hers!

The actress Gemma Craven tells how one of her early misdeeds greatly embarrassed her mother. When she was about five her mother had a friend to tea, a friend who gave Gemma a massive bag of sweets. She staggered out into the street and rounded up all her playmates, letting each of them touch and admire the bag, but they were not allowed to have one. Then she went back into the house and returned the bag to her mother's friend, saying, 'Thank you. You can have it back now. I've shown it to all my friends, but they are the kind of sweets I really hate.'

Sir Godfrey Agnew tells how when he was six, the family lived in Kenya. He must have overheard his parents discussing a friend who was coming for lunch, for half-way through the meal, when his mother rebuked him for staring at the friend, he defended himself by saying, 'But Mummy, he does not drink like a fish at all.'

The American poet Carl Sandburg once took his little daughter to Springfield, Illinois, to visit Abraham Lincoln's tomb. The custodian showed them through the building. A number of other visitors had gathered beside the tomb. They all stood in silent reverence. Then suddenly his daughter pulled at his coat sleeve and said in a voice loud enough to be heard by all, 'Daddy, when are they going to roll the stone away?'

A Bishop once delivered an address at a large church. He told several sparkling anecdotes, but because he wished to repeat them at later meetings, he asked the reporters not to include any of them in their reports. The Bishop and his family were considerably embarrassed when they read one report. After giving a concise summary of his address, the young reporter had added, 'The Bishop also told a number of stories that cannot be published.'

A former national convenor of the Church of Scotland's 'Temperance and Morals Committee' holidayed annually with his wife in Newtonmore. At that time, Newtonmore was a favourite holiday resort for ministers. At that time also, the main concerns of the Temperance and Morals Committee were 'drink' and 'gambling'. Mr ... had been appointed convenor just before he went on holiday. What a ragging he received from several of his ministerial colleagues with whom he golfed regularly on holiday. Knowing that he enjoyed the occasional sherry, they inquired whether he was going to change his ways, or whether they could expect to see a change in the church's policy with regard to drink. 'I agree drink is a problem,' he said, 'but the real curse is gambling. That will certainly be my main concern.' Three hours later as they were approaching the 18th green, the minister's daughter came rushing out from the clubhouse. 'Daddy,' she said, 'you will never guess what has happened. Mummy has won the jackpot in the one-armed bandit in the clubhouse.' His friends could scarcely restrain a chuckle, but her father was not amused. Noticing his face drop, his daughter said, 'Don't worry, Dad. She's not keeping the money. She's buying drinks for everyone.'

In his autobiography, Cardinal Heenan tells how his parents were persuaded to enter a competition organised by their local parish priest. A prize was to be awarded by the church to a couple who had not had a cross word for a year. After Mass one Whit Monday, the priest called his father into the sacristy and told him to enter the competition. He was aghast, for he knew nothing would induce his wife to make an exhibition of herself. Then the priest revealed that there was only one other couple and that they too had been coerced into entering. Mr Heenan went home disconsolate to persuade his wife that it was the will of God that they enter. That afternoon, his father went into the witness box and declared brazenly that he and his wife had not had a cross word during the past year, or indeed throughout their married life. He said he was a very even-tempered man and that his wife was the sweetest natured woman in the world. So far so good. When his wife was brought to the witness stand, she too was asked, 'When did you last have a quarrel with your husband?' 'This morning,' she replied, 'when he told me I had to go in for this awful competition.'

A Mr Cook tells how his father, having taped their wedding service, sat down quietly one night to add an introduction to the recording. He had just started, when the door-bell rang. Opening the door he found the local vicar. Mr Cook's father invited him to listen to the recording. He switched on the machine. After a few seconds, there was the sound of the doorbell, followed clearly by the exclamation, 'Blast it! Who the Hell is that?'

One day when a minister and his wife were entertaining friends, their son John came in from playing, to join them for a meal. He was immediately despatched to the bathroom to wash his hands. 'You know what I keep saying about germs, Johnnie,' said his mother. From outside the dining room door, a little voice was clearly heard to mutter, 'Germs and Jesus. It's all I hear about in this house, and I've never seen either.'

A Family Christmas

There are three periods in a person's life:
1. When you believe in Santa Claus.
2. When you don't believe in Santa Claus.
3. When you are Santa Claus.

❦

An English teacher took her little son to see Santa for the first time. 'If that is Santa Claus,' he asked bewildered, 'who are all the other men with white beards on the street?' Quickly drawing on her classroom experience, she explained, 'Oh, these are subordinate clauses.'

❦

During a lull in the proceedings, the store Santa was given a cup of coffee. Just then, a nine-year-old boy came into the grotto. Santa began by asking the lad if he believed in Santa Claus. When he said he no longer did, Santa said, 'That's fine. I can take my beard off. It's much easier to drink coffee without it.'

❦

One little boy, more honest than most, said, 'Everybody loves baby Jesus, but I don't. I love the three wise men because they brought presents.'

❦

In a radio phone-in programme the little girl who was speaking to Santa insisted on having a final word. 'Santa, would you please put my presents up high so that my wee brother can't get them.'

❦

Mr Day recalls an incident from his youth. His father, a former pipe-smoker, was sitting reading the paper. His young brother lay on the floor busily making a Father

Christmas out of crepe paper and cotton wool. Suddenly, the wee lad asked, 'Does Santa smoke a pipe?' 'He used to,' said his father, 'but your mother stopped him.'

🦖

John and Tom were brothers, but very different in nature and outlook. John was a pessimist, Tom an optimist. It concerned the parents that the boys were so different. They wanted to redress the balance. Christmas was approaching, so on Christmas Eve they filled John's stocking full of fruit, sweets, money and many other goodies that go into Christmas stockings. At the foot of Tom's stocking they put some horse manure. The following morning they eagerly awaited the boys' reactions. John appeared first, but he was not all smiles as they had expected. The tangerine had stones, the sweets were not the right kind, and there was not nearly enough money to buy what he wanted. When Tom appeared, to their great surprise, he was smiling. 'I haven't seen it yet,' he said, 'but I'm sure I got a pony.'

🦖

Perhaps someone should add a thirteenth verse to the song *The Twelve Days of Christmas*.

On the thirteenth day of Christmas
My true love sent to me,
Ten Dispirin, One Massive Overdraft and the last of the turkey.

🦖

Christmas cards can sometimes present problems.

'We sent them one last year and they didn't send us one, so they probably won't send us one this year, because they will think we won't send them one, because they didn't last year, don't you think – or shall we?'

🦖

Opening a card which read 'From Annie and Eddie,' the wife said to her husband, 'I know an Annie but her man isn't Eddie, and I know an Eddie but his wife isn't Annie.'

Late one November, a little girl was taken shopping in Glasgow by her mother. Although the Christmas decorations and lights had been erected in George Square, the lights were not yet on. Her mother explained that soon the Lord Provost would switch them on. One morning a week later, they were back in the city centre. Being daylight the lights were naturally not on. The wee girl was very upset. Not only her faith in her Mum, but her faith in God, was being sorely tried. 'Mummy,' she said, 'you said the Lord promised to switch the lights on.'

Judi Dench tells how several weeks before Christmas her young daughter returned from school and excitedly told her they were putting on a play at school. When Judi enquired what the play was about, she was told it was about the inn-keeper's wife. Trying to hide her surprise Judi then asked if she had a part in the play. 'Yes,' she said, 'I am the inn-keeper's wife.' Her daughter was convinced that the main character in the play was not Mary or Joseph, or the baby Jesus, but the inn-keeper's wife!

A Primary School teacher was discussing the Nativity with her class. They talked about which animals might have been in the stable. One child suggested cows, another a donkey, another oxen, a fourth a 'stable bear'.

A teacher, having told the children the Bethlehem story, asked them how they imagined Mary would feel in the stable. One wee girl said she would probably be feeling poorly because of the bump on her head. Surprised by her

62

answer, the teacher asked how she thought Mary had a bump on her head. 'Because you said that when the innkeeper opened the door the light fell on Mary.'

What children hear in carols and the Nativity story is not always quite accurate.

Away in a manger no crib for a bed
The little Lord Jesus laid down his wee Ted.

Once in oil was David sitting.

A little six-year-old was upset because she had not been chosen to be the 'Virgin Fairy' in the school Nativity play.

When the little girl asked her pregnant mother where she was going to lay her baby, the mother pointed out that mummies were not birds, that babies are not laid. 'But Mummy,' she replied, 'the minister said Mary laid Jesus in a manger.'

Children's definitions of Christmas:

Christmas is making a secret present for your Dad at school, which is always a calendar.
Christmas is hearing about those partridges in pear trees, until you are ready to go insane.
Christmas is getting all those cards from people you never sent one to.
Christmas is when you hug your little brother.
Christmas is when we receive lots of presents we cannot wait to exchange.

A wealthy businessman once asked his friend Leigh Hodges, 'Guess what I am giving my boy for Christmas?' Expecting it to be some costly present, Hodges was surprised when the man handed him a paper on which was written: 'To my dear son. I give you one hour of each weekday and two hours of my Sundays, to be used as you wish. Your Father.' Leigh Hodges later commented, 'It is the greatest gift a man can give.'

A primary teacher had informed her class that the following day the Chaplain was coming to conduct the Christmas service. At the appointed time, she led her pupils along the corridor to the school hall. The collection plate, which was at the door of the hall, was causing quite a hold-up. The chaplain, who was standing with the headmaster watching the children file past, spoke to some of the boys who had stopped beside him. He began by asking them if they knew his name. He expected them to say Mr R... but instead, one wee lad said, 'You are the chaplain.' 'That's right,' he said, 'but do you know my other name?' 'Please sir,' said one, 'is it Charlie?'

Every year in his church in Port Glasgow, Father Simon Keane set up a Nativity scene with life-sized figures. In the manger was a lovely doll representing the baby Jesus. One night as he went into the church to switch on the lights, he heard a baby crying. The cry seemed to be coming from the manger. Tiptoeing forward, he discovered that there was a real baby in the manger. As he lifted the child he caught sight of a little girl cradling the doll-like figure of the baby Jesus. There was a look of infinite tenderness on her face. As the priest approached her she said apologetically, 'I just wanted to hold the baby Jesus, so I laid my wee brother in the manger so that it wouldn't be empty.'

One Christmas a man received a beautifully wrapped packet from his wife. Inside was a home-made gift voucher. He read it, and read it again. Then he nearly fell over backwards. It said, 'Gift to be delivered on or around 10th August.' The baby duly arrived.

A little boy had bought his grandmother a Bible for Christmas. He wanted to write a suitable inscription on the flyleaf. He thought and thought until suddenly he remembered that his father had a book with an inscription in it, a book of which he was very proud. The wee lad decided to copy it. When Grandma opened her gift on Christmas morning, she found neatly inscribed, 'To Grandma with the compliments of the author.'

The minister of an American Presbyterian Church tells how the ten-year-olds directed and acted the Christmas story. It opened with the scene at the inn. Joseph and Mary arrived and asked for a room.

Innkeeper: 'Can't you see the "No vacancy" sign?'

Joseph: 'Yes, but can't you see my wife's expecting a baby any minute?'

Innkeeper: 'Well, that's not my fault!'

Joseph: 'Well, it's not mine either.'

James T. Cleland's father and austere mother disapproved of all Sunday amusements. The Sunday after Christmas, James gathered all the toy soldiers which he had received for Christmas around him. He was getting ready for a mock battle, when suddenly he saw his mother standing in the doorway with a frown spreading over her face. In a flash James responded, 'Look, the Salvation Army.'

Fighting on the Beaches

Churchill's famous words sound rather like many a family holiday: 'We shall fight on the beaches, we shall fight on the landing grounds, we shall fight in the fields and in the streets, we shall fight in the hills.'

🐾

A holiday is when you pack seven suitcases, three small children, a mother-in-law, two dogs and say, 'It's good to get away from it all.'

🐾

It's hard to settle down when you come back from holiday and sometimes even harder to settle up.

🐾

A family were going on holiday with their two children to the Canary Islands. During the flight, the four-year-old was invited up to the flight deck. When he returned to his seat, he exclaimed, 'Mummy, the pilot's going to the Canary Islands as well.'

🐾

A luggage-laden husband stared miserably down the platform at the departing train. 'If you had not taken so long to get ready,' he said to his wife, 'we could have caught it.' 'Yes,' she replied, 'and if you had not hurried me so, we wouldn't have to wait so long for the next one.'

🐾

One mother was telling another about their hotel problems when they were on holiday. 'The food was poison – and such small portions.'

🐾

You can't always believe what a tourist guide tells you. A guide, who was taking American tourists on a conducted tour of Edinburgh's Royal Mile, stopped the bus outside the house of the sixteenth-century reformer, John Knox. Pointing to the house, he said, 'This is the home of the famous John Knox.' From the back of the bus, one of the party asked, 'And who was John Knox?' With a look of disgust on his face, the Scottish guide turned to the man and said, 'Have you never read your Bible?'

A Mr Wright tells of staying in a small-town hotel. The first morning he made the mistake of ordering morning tea. Shortly before seven, a girl threw open the door. 'Sugar in your tea?' she shouted. 'No thank you,' he replied. Before she banged the door shut, she said, 'Don't stir it then.'

In a letter to *TV Times*, a Mr McQueen tells how, during a tour of the Scottish Highlands, he and his wife booked into a guest house for dinner, bed and breakfast. The landlady made them very welcome. She inquired if they had any likes or dislikes about food. They assured her they were not fussy. When she then asked if they liked porridge, his wife replied that they did, but not to make it specially for them. 'Oh it's no bother,' she said, 'I make it for the dog anyway.'

A couple who were about to sail from Scrabster to Orkney across the stormy Pentland Firth, asked the Captain what he would recommend for sea sickness. 'Tak whisky,' he said, 'you'll enjoy it both as it goes down and as it comes up!'

If you really look like your passport photograph, then you certainly need a holiday.

A Glasgow man watching Arnold Palmer hit a monstrous drive during the Open at Troon, turned to his wife and said as the ball went screaming away into the distance, 'Jean, that man hits his drives farther than we go on our holidays.'

After hearing her mother describe the family's camping holiday enthusiastically to a friend, the small daughter remarked thoughtfully, 'That sounds more fun than it really was.'

Who says you can't have it both ways? On holiday in Britain, you often get off-season weather at high-season rates.

Two women were discussing their forthcoming holidays. When one mentioned she was going to Tenerife, the other said, 'Where's that?' 'Oh, I don't know,' she replied. 'We're going by air.'

There was a delightful misprint on the menu of a holiday restaurant. Consecutive items on the menu were 'Scampi £6.50. Scimpi half-portion £3.20.'

The sign on a butcher's shop greatly amused some holidaymakers: 'Try our steak pies. You won't get better.'

A Highland worthy who was certainly not impressed by what he saw on television of the hair-styles and 'mod' clothes of the young people in London, was once asked if he had ever seen the sights of London and Paris. 'No,' he replied, 'And I have no desire to. Enough of these sights come here every year.'

❧

A wife was overheard saying to a friend, 'When we go on holiday, if my husband gets lost, it is the map that is wrong. If I get lost it is because I cannot read the map.'

❧

A former golfing friend told me that now when he goes on holiday, he paints watercolours rather than plays golf. 'It is not only cheaper: I require fewer strokes!'

❧

On returning from a holiday abroad an American woman was asked by her priest if she had visited the Holy Land. 'We sure did,' she said. 'My husband just had to play St Andrews.'

❧

Notice in Travel Agent's window: 'Please do us a favour and GO AWAY.'

❧

A notice in a holiday brochure about a certain hotel described it as being in the shadiest part of the town. 'You cannot fail to remark upon the odours of the pine-trees and our swimming pool.'

❧

Another read: 'All the water used in this hotel for cooking has been passed by the manager personally.'

❧

Inquiring about holiday accommodation in a remote area of West Ireland, a Belfast businessman received a letter with the following information: 'The private bathroom does not contain a toilet, but the room has a balcony overlooking the sea.'

❧

A cartoon depicted two women outside a Glasgow Bingo Hall. The one was saying to the other, 'To think that last night we were playing Bingo in Majorca.'

❧

'When visiting lands the brochures call exotic,
It's best to have some pills, anti-biotic.'

❧

The Rev Dr Murdo Ewan Macdonald tells how he and his family were once on holiday on the island of Lewis. The house was in a secluded spot near the beach. They came in fact to regard it as their own private beach. From time to time, other holiday makers would come down the path past their house to the beach. During a light-hearted family discussion concerning how they might prevent others using their 'private' beach, one of the boys, a typical minister's son, suggested that they might erect a notice at the end of the path, which would read, 'Religious Service in progress. All welcome.'

❧

Beside a soft-drink stand was a notice, 'Thirst come, thirst served'.

❧

One father on his return from a Spanish holiday complained that the beach had been so crowded he had spent most of his holiday in other people's snaps.

Another father used to say that one of the wonderful things about a holiday is that it makes you feel good enough to go back to work, and poor enough so that you have to.

It was Bob Hope who said there was nothing quite like a British summer, except perhaps an Arctic winter.

A Mr Waterhouse tells of going to a travel agent's to book a holiday. In front of him was a man with his elbows on the counter. He was obviously in no hurry. He wasn't sure whether he wanted to go to Tenerife or Villefranche, and he could only go on the second Thursday in July or the first Wednesday in August. He wanted half-board with vegetarian meals, and a connecting flight from Edinburgh for his mother-in-law. Mr Waterhouse was absolutely sure that come holiday time that man, or some relative of his, would be standing in front of him at the airport check-in desk. He would have an overweight suitcase and an out-of-date passport.

Prince Charles did part of his schooling in Australia. One Sunday, unannounced, he attended the local church. At the end of the service, the minister apologised for the poor attendance. 'Being bank holiday weekend most of the members are away.' 'Not another bank holiday!' said the prince. 'What's this one for?' Slightly embarrassed the minister replied, 'In Australia we call it the Queen's birthday.'

The Family Pew

An old lady and a very small boy were seated side by side in a church pew. As the collection plate was being passed, the wee lad noticed that the lady seemed to be fumbling in her pockets. Leaning over, he whispered, 'Here, you take my 50p. I can hide under the seat.'

When the minister asked the children why coffee was served at the close of the service, one boy suggested, 'Is it to get people wide awake before they drive home?' Another minister got an equally unexpected reply when he asked, 'How long do you think Adam and Eve were in the Garden of Eden before being expelled?' 'At least until September,' said one wee lad, 'because that is when the apples are ripe.'

A little Presbyterian boy, in an Anglican Church for the first time, watched wide-eyed as the choirboys filed in, clad in their white surplices. With wonder in his voice, he turned to his mother and said, 'Are all these boys going to get their hair cut?'

A priest hearing children's confessions was puzzled to find child after child confessing to 'throwing peanuts in the river'. He wondered whether they were repenting of wasting school food, or of river pollution. He decided he would ask the next boy to explain, but the next boy didn't make the same confession. When the youngster finished, the priest said, 'Is that all you have to confess? Have you not forgotten something? What about throwing peanuts in the river?' 'But Father,' said a bewildered little voice, 'I am Peanuts.'

Several years ago during a Harvest service in an Ayrshire church, one little boy came forward and handed the minister his tray of fruit. The minister noticed under the cling-foil there were two apples, two bananas, two oranges, one pear and the core of a pear!

❧

A bishop was astonished to hear little Mary say that a person must be brave these days to go to church. 'Why do you say that?' asked the bishop. 'Well I heard my uncle tell my aunt last Sunday that there was a canon in the pulpit, that the choir murdered the anthem, and that the organist drowned the choir.'

❧

Abraham Lincoln once told how as children they all used to be made to stand in a long line and read the scriptures aloud. 'One day our lesson was about the faithful Israelites who were thrown into the fiery furnace and were delivered by the Lord. One little fellow had to read the verses in which appeared for the first time the names Shadrach, Meschach and Abednego. The boy stumbled on Shadrach, floundered on Meschach and went all to pieces on Abednego. Instantly the hand of the teacher gave him a cuff on the head that left him wailing and blubbering as the next boy in line went on with the reading. By the time the first round was over, he had quietened down and stopped sniffling.

'His blunder and disgrace were forgotten by the others in the class until it was almost his turn to read again. Suddenly he sent up a wail which alarmed even the teacher, who with rather unusual gentleness asked, "What's the matter now?" Pointing with a shaking finger at the verse which he was soon to read, the boy managed to stammer, "Look teacher, here come these three fellows again".'

❧

The Rev Richard Davis tells how he was once sitting in the living room reading the newspaper. His three-year-old son was sprawled in front of him, absorbed in a building project, using his wooden blocks. His concentration was intense. Finally Mr Davis said, 'Ben, what are you building?'

'Sssshhhhhh...' he responded, a finger to his lips and a scolding look on his face. 'Quiet Dad, I'm making a church.' 'That's great Ben, but why do I have to be quiet?' 'Because people are sleeping, and we don't want to waken them.'

'Of course ministers' kids tend to be wild and unruly,' admitted one minister. 'They have to play with the children in the congregation, don't they?'

A young minister, speaking to the children one day about coping with disappointments and irritations, used the analogy of Andrew the Oyster who got a little bit of grit inside him. He told the children how Andrew coped with it, how he covered the irritation with one silky coat after another. Having elaborated at some length on this, he then asked the children if any of them could tell him what finally happened. The answer he got wasn't quite what he expected. 'They probably killed Andrew to get the pearl out.'

The Rev Doug Ibach tells of an Advent service he will never forget. In his talk to the children, he asked what special time of year it was. To his amazement, one little boy, Kelly, said, 'Easter.' Fortunately the other children knew it was Advent. He then went on to talk about the meaning of Advent. Before the children left the church to go to their Sunday School classes, he wished them all a happy Advent. He then added (later regretting it), 'And I wish Kelly a Happy Easter.' When Kelly got to the door of the Church, he turned, and in a loud voice shouted out, 'And a happy Hallowe'en to you.' Later that week, Kelly's mother, who had still not fully recovered from the experience, phoned Mr Ibach to inform him that her husband was being moved to Chicago. 'You will be glad to know,' she said, 'that Kelly is coming with us.'

A lady tells how her seven-year-old grandson asked her one day, 'Grandma, what church do we go to?' When she replied 'The Episcopal', he said, 'Oh I told them at school we went to the Despicable.'

Writing in the *Baptist Times*, a Baptist minister told how at their Sunday School, the young people were encouraged to collect pennies in Smartie tubes for children facing starvation. One of the children who had just been given a £1 coin by his grandma decided to put it in. His parents tried to explain that £1 was a lot of money and how his gran wanted him to save it for his holiday. They explained that he was only expected to put pennies into his Smartie tube. 'But you don't understand,' he answered. 'Those children are very hungry.'

One of my favourite ecumenical stories concerns infant baptism. It indicates that the differences between the churches are not as great as they seem!

A Methodist minister and a Baptist minister were having a great argument. The Baptist minister insisted a person had to be baptised by total immersion. The Methodist in an effort to compromise said, 'Suppose I go in knee deep?' 'That does not count,' said the Baptist minister. 'Suppose I go in chin deep?' 'No, it has to be all the way.' 'Aha,' said the Methodist minister. 'Just as I thought. It is only the water that is on the child's head that counts!'

One little boy, who was asked why he thought the priest in the story of the Good Samaritan passed by on the other side, said, 'Because the man lying by the roadside had already been robbed.'

A number of little boys were being sternly questioned by the minister's wife about the mysterious disappearance of some fruit from her back garden. 'Do you know,' she said, 'what the Bible says about thieves?' One boy, better versed in Scripture than the others, replied, 'Please Ma'am, "Today thou shalt be with me in Paradise".'

The Rev. G. B. Wilcox tells how he was once endeavouring to explain to children the nature of faith. 'I told the familiar story of a child on board a ship. A pet monkey snatches the boy's cap and darts with it up into the rigging. The little fellow makes after it, climbing higher and higher until at last the sailors, to their horror, see him far up at a point where he is growing dizzy and is just about to pitch headlong to the deck. His father, summoned from his cabin, shouts to him to leap up and out into the water. The child hesitates, but finally trusting his father's wisdom, makes the tremendous leap and is brought up safely from the water by the sailors. One little chap in the class, as I was telling the story as vividly as possible, seemed very impressed and sat deeply thinking as I made the application. The truth seemed to have taken hold. A hopeful case, I thought. At last he couldn't contain himself any longer. "Sir, what happened to the monkey?"'

Bishop Sheen remembers whilst preaching once in a little country church, a mother, embarrassed by her crying child, made to leave the church. 'Madam,' said the bishop, 'it's quite all right. The child isn't bothering me.' 'I know,' replied the mother, 'but you're bothering the child.'

The kiss at the wedding ceremony was a rather long one. Finally a child's voice rang out in the silence of the church. 'Mummy, is he spreading the pollen over her now?'

Buy – Buy

The person who says money does not matter is either a fool or a liar.

An Aberdeenshire farmer, James Nicol, made his fortune in Angus cattle. He later purchased and presented to the Church of Scotland a hotel at Stonehaven. His idea was that the Church would run it as an eventide home, and that he and his elderly sister might spend the latter years of their life there. The Church agreed, calling the home after his farm, 'Clashfarquhar'.

A young reporter from the *Press and Journal* sought an interview with Mr Nicol. During the interview the reporter asked how he, a young man of twenty-four, could set about becoming a millionaire. 'Are you married?' inquired Mr Nicol. When the reporter said he was, the old man smiled ruefully and said, 'Well son, you don't have a chance.'

'My wife,' said one man sadly, 'is like a baby. She always wants to go buy–buy.'

A man tells how the day before his wife's birthday he set out to buy her a present. Aware of his intentions, she said, 'Don't buy me anything practical. It's the impractical things I really need.'

A cunning wife asks for something she knows her husband can't afford, so she can compromise and get what she really wants.

A husband worried about how he was going to pay all his bills received a sympathetic kiss from his wife. 'Look on the bright side dear,' she said. 'We could be poor instead of just broke.'

The feeling that your home is your castle is strongest when you get an estimate to have it painted.

'You could describe my financial situation as being fluid,' said one harassed husband, 'which is really another way of saying I'm going down the drain.'

A British poll organisation, that feels the public pulse on timely topics, asked members of the middle class, 'Given a one tenth reduction in income, where would you make the cuts?' One depressed country teacher replied, 'Across my throat.'

Two in a restaurant,
Romeo and Juliet
He had no cash to pay the debt,
So Romeo'd what Juliet.

A Scottish family who had dined out one night in London were appalled at the size of the bill. Calling the English waiter, the father said, 'If you English had charged like this at Bannockburn, you might have won.'

A farm-hand who had married a rich wife bought a lovely house and farm. The wife filled the house with lovely furniture. The husband bought cows, sheep, pigs, horses. He also built great barns. One day they took friends on a conducted tour of the house and the farm. Seeing how proud her husband was, showing off his livestock, she said, 'Remember John, if it hadn't been for my money you would never have had all this.'

'I agree,' said John, 'but remember that if it had not been for your money, you would never have had me.'

The little girl was keen that her father should see the notice in the pet shop, a notice relating to some puppies in a cage. 'Who says money can't buy happiness?'

A wife tells how her husband who had inherited quite a sum of money decided to buy a new house and change the car. She was surprised when, having just bought a brand-new house, he returned the following day with an old Jaguar. 'Why didn't you buy a new car and let our new neighbours see we are quite well off?' He replied, 'I deliberately bought the four-year-old Jaguar so that they will think we have always been quite well off.'

Many of Bob's friends were amazed when after smoking heavily for twenty years, he gave up completely. Often he would talk to his old father about his 'conversion' to non-smoking. Eventually his father said, 'Bob, when you were a boy I remember offering you £50 if you would not smoke, but you started smoking. Then I offered you £50 if you would stop, but you kept on. Now that you have stopped, I will give you £50 if you will stop talking about it.'

The problem with some families is that the net income of the parents does not keep up with their gross habits.

A couple who were settling in and trying to settle up, were discussing the future. 'Some day Mary, we will be rich and have a lot of money.' 'John', she said, 'we are rich. Some day we may have money.' She knew the real measure of our wealth is how much we'd be worth if we lost all our money!

The Cost of Living in Creases

As I look in the mirror I see,
And my wondering never ceases
How year after year I receive
My cost of living in creases.

Father time is a great artist, but many do not care for the lines he draws.

A middle-aged lady in the Post Office was given a form to complete. Filling in her name and address presented no problem. But when she came to the little box with the word AGE, she hesitated. She looked around to make sure no one was looking, then hesitated again. Finally the man behind the counter leant across and said, 'Madam, the longer you wait the worse it gets.'

Do those getting married seem to you like children?
Do your children now prefer company of their own choosing? Do you call a radio, a 'wireless'?
Do you find it increasingly difficult to read the telephone directory?
Does your weight-lifting consist now mainly of standing up?
Do you find that clothes you have not recently worn, have shrunk?
Do you find no humour in the slogan, 'Bald is beautiful'?
Do you grudge paying the barber the full amount for trimming the hair round your bald patch?
Does your mind immediately calculate calories when presented with a menu?
Do you know only the names of the coaches and managers when you take your youngsters to a football match?

Do you interpret every bout of indigestion as advance warning of a coronary?

Do you find you can't think of anything when your wife asks what you would like to do on your birthday?

Do you no longer look for greener fields, finding it difficult enough to mow the one you've got?

Do the wrinkles you see in the mirror disappear when you take off your glasses?

IF SO, THE LIKELIHOOD IS YOU ARE MIDDLE-AGED.

Failing memory is another common characteristic of middle age. A minister who was concerned about his ability to remember names and appointments, noticed one day in a bookshop a volume entitled, *How to Improve Your Memory*. On returning home he went to put it in the appropriate section of his library. Having done this he noticed next to it a book he had purchased the previous year. The title, *How to Improve Your Memory*.

There may be something in the idea of reincarnation. Some women of forty can remember things that happened forty-five years before.

A cartoon depicted a dejected looking man sitting at a public bar. The barman is saying to him, 'OK so you're forty. You've lived half your life. But look on the bright side. If you were a horse you would already be dead more than fifteen years.'

We all have three ages: a chronological age marked by the calendar; a biological age programmed to our genes and blood pressure; a psychological age programmed to our mental outlook.

Some people are never young. On one schoolboy's report the headmaster had entered the comment, 'Would make an excellent father.' Others are never middle-aged. A prolonged adolescence merges into a premature senility! Our psychological age affects our biological age. Growing older is inevitable, but how quickly we grow old is determined by our thoughts, interests and enthusiasm. The famous beauty expert Helena Rubenstein once remarked, 'I have never had my face lifted. I prefer to have my spirits lifted. The effect is much the same.'

One of the frightening things about middle age is that you grow out of it.

A woman said that for her the one advantage of middle age is that she can no longer read the bathroom scales.

Youth tends to look ahead. Old age tends to look back. Middle age tends to look worried.

The secret of staying young is to eat properly, sleep sufficiently, exercise properly – and lie about your age.

A middle-aged couple tell how one night their teenage son, who had just passed his driving test, asked for the car. All night they worried about the lad. They visibly jumped when the phone rang about midnight. It was the nurse in the hospital casualty ward. 'There's been a car accident,' she said. 'One of the people involved has asked me to tell you not to worry. He is going to be all right.' 'Oh thank God,' said the husband. Then the nurse continued, 'It's your father.' They were worrying about the wrong generation.

Ills, Pills and Wills

Richard Needham defined the seven ages of man as spills, drills, thrills, bills, ills, pills and wills.

Age gives people away. It tells on them.

The aging process is a great reminder that if your goal is to maintain the status quo, you will fail.

Old men give good advice to compensate for no longer being able to give a bad example.

When a Highlander was asked to what he attributed his long life, he replied, 'Regular breathing. Once you have stopped breathing, you've had it.'

Another old worthy when asked how he was, replied, 'I'm still walking about. It saves funeral expenses.'

The irony of life is that by the time you are old enough to know your way around, you are not going anywhere – or if you do get to greener pastures, you can't climb the fence.

A man tells how after being retired for a couple of years and completing all the jobs his wife had lined up for him to do, he decided to enrol for a course at the local adult education college. He had been told that pensioners did not have to pay a fee. Handing in the completed form, he announced to the secretary, 'I'm sixty-seven.' Then pulling out his wallet, he asked if she wanted to see his birth certificate. 'No, that's all right,' she said. 'Oh, do I look honest?' he asked her. 'No,' she replied, 'you look sixty-seven.'

In a depressed moment one man said, 'Age improves wine, compound interest, and nothing else.' Another said, 'I don't feel eighty. In fact I don't feel anything until noon. Then it's time for my nap.'

The ancient proverb, 'Whom the gods love die young', did not mean what many think it means, that those whom the gods love are taken from this life in their youth. It meant that those whom the gods love retain the gift of essential youth even when well on in years. In other words, the great art of living is to die young as late as possible.

Dr Ernest Sangster argued that beauty competitions should be held only for people over seventy years of age. 'When you are young,' he said, 'you have the face and figure that God gave you, but when you are seventy, you have the face and figure you have partly made for yourself.' He knew that beautiful young people are accidents of nature but beautiful old people are works of art.

Contrary to public opinion, many old folk do *not* grow old gracefully. People only grow old gracefully if they were gracious in their earlier years. The officer-in-charge of the Dornoch Eventide Home tells how one of the residents was most reluctant each morning to get up and come down for breakfast. Going into her room one morning, he said, as nicely as possible, 'Come on, get up. You're getting lazy.' Smiling, she replied, 'No I'm not. I've always been lazy.' People's dominant characteristics do tend to become more dominant the older they become.

A resident in another eventide home who had just celebrated her ninetieth birthday, said to her minister, 'You will never guess what my grandson gave me for my birthday. He gave me a five-year diary.' Then she added, 'You really cannot let down such faith in you.'

Finlay Currie, the well-known Scottish actor, continued to act well into his eighties. On a radio chat show shortly before he died at the age of ninety, the interviewer went over his distinguished career in acting. When he inquired whether Finlay had ever played a romantic lead, Finlay replied, 'Not yet. Not yet.' What wonderful spirit.

It was little different with the late Methodist Bishop Herbert Welsh, who died in America at the age of one hundred and seven. He retained his love of life and sense of humour right up to the end. We are told how one day towards the end of his life, he got to complaining about certain things. He said in his early days he had been a missionary, and just after he had left the mission field they raised the salary of missionaries. He was then elected a bishop, and the year after he retired they raised the salaries of bishops. 'Now,' he said, 'the girls are wearing miniskirts and I am going blind.'

Sometimes when old folk dress in unconventional ways, or are not over-concerned about what they wear, they are diagnosed by amateur psychiatrists as becoming senile. But if this is the criterion for senility, surely we would have to certify many young people who dress like scarecrows.

An unknown elderly gentleman once penned the following lines under the heading *Sad but True*:

Everything is farther away than it used to be. It is twice as far to the shop now, and I notice they have added a hill. I have given up running for the bus for it leaves faster than it used to. It seems that they are making the stairs steeper than in the old days.

Have you noticed the print is smaller in the paper now? There is no sense in asking anyone to read aloud; everyone speaks with such a low voice these days, I can hardly hear them. And the material in clothes is so skimpy, especially round the waist. Even people are changing. They are so much younger now than they used to be when I was their age. On the other hand people of my own age are so much older than I am.

I met an old classmate in the street the other day and she had aged so badly that she did not even know me. I got to thinking about the poor old soul this morning and, in doing so, glanced at my reflection in my new mirror. Really, they just don't make good mirrors any more, do they?

❧

The older you get the further you had to walk to school as a child.

❧

'Cheer up,' said one old man to his friend. 'You have two chances – one of getting the disease and one of not. And if you get the disease you have two chances, one of dying and one of not. And if you die, well, you still have two chances.'

❧

Dean Ramsay in his *Scottish Life and Character* tells the story of old Mrs Robinson who could not bear affected piety. When an elderly gentleman she had invited to dinner accepted with the reservation, 'If I'm spared,' she retorted, 'Well, if you're deid, I'll no expect you.'

❧

When Lord Palmerston's doctor broke the news to the elderly statesman that he was going to die, he replied, 'Die, that's the last thing I'm going to do.'

Grave Matters

'Where there's a will there's a wail.'

🐾

Death is nature's way of telling you to slow down.

🐾

An undertaker tells how he sometimes gets a letter from a close family friend. He always signs himself, 'Eventually Yours.'

🐾

An 'Acknowledgement' notice in a paper read, 'Mrs Smith wishes to thank the nurses and doctor for their kind cooperation in the loss of her husband.'

🐾

An elderly couple in a restaurant had obviously been to a funeral. They were discussing the rival merits of cremation and burial. Suddenly the wife said to the husband, 'John, you have never said whether you'd like to be cremated or buried?' 'Surprise me,' he said.

🐾

A news item in the *Daily Telegraph* told how dying is to cost more in Norfolk. Higher burial charges were to be introduced. The report then added, 'The increased cost of *living* is to blame.'

🐾

An employer is reported to have asked one of the office-boys if he believed in life after death. When the boy said he did, his employer said, 'That certainly helps. About half an hour after you left yesterday to attend your grandfather's funeral, he came into the office to see you.'

🐾

The Biblical question, 'If a man die shall he live again?' is one that most families ask at some time or another. A BBC producer who was preparing two satirical programmes on heaven and hell, wrote to the corporation's Catholic consultant asking how he could get the official Roman Catholic view. The consultant wrote back: 'DIE.'

❦

At one time it was taken as a great offence among neighbours if you were not invited to a funeral. Two sisters, who felt themselves slighted in this way, watched from the window as the funeral went past. 'Well, never mind. We'll be upsides with them yet. We will have a funeral of our own some day.'

❦

Drive carefully. Why die in perfect health?

❦

In Glasgow the phrase 'Awa tae Hell' is one of the meaningless phrases which people use when they hear some surprising piece of news. My father loved to tell of a conversation which he overheard on an old Glasgow tram. The two ladies sitting in front of him had obviously not met for some time. 'How's your husband?' said one. 'Oh he died last week,' replied the other. 'Awa tae Hell,' said the first, obviously upset. 'Aye, last Tuesday.'

❦

An Eddie Russell tells of applying for a post with Queen Margaret University in Edinburgh. The application form asked him to tick the reason for leaving his previous job. He was slightly nonplussed on noticing that one of the options was 'died in service'. He said he could only assume this applied to those looking for a dead-end job!

❦

Two local worthies were discussing the virtues and shortcomings of an old fellow who had just died. One of the men asked the other if he would be going to the funeral. 'No,' he replied, 'He's not coming to mine, so I'm not going to his.'

When Winston Churchill was informed one day in the House of Commons that Aneurin Bevan, his great political rival, had just died, Churchill bowed his head, clearly shaken. 'A great man, a brilliant man. A tragic loss,' he muttered. Some minutes later another MP came to his front-bench post to inform him that the Press was waiting outside to get his 'heartfelt opinions on Nye Bevan'. Churchill thought for a moment, then looked up warily and said, 'Are you quite sure he is dead?'

When Konrad Adenauer, the first chancellor of the German Federal Republic, was in his late eighties and still chancellor, he caught a heavy cold. His doctor, unable to be of much help, had to put up with Adenauer's impatience. 'I'm not a magician,' he said. 'I cannot make you young again.' 'I don't want you to,' retorted the chancellor. 'All I want is to go on getting older.'

Though Anna and Jennie were sisters, they had not spoken to each other for more than twenty years. Their niece Betty recalled how when Anna died, Jennie attended her funeral. When asked why she had come when they hadn't spoken for so long, she replied, 'And I didn't speak to her today either.'

Before James Rodgers was to be shot in 1960 in Nevada he was asked if he had a last request. 'Yes, a bullet-proof vest.' Despite his wit, his request was not granted.

A Wick grave-digger once informed a lady visitor to Caithness that where he worked he had more people 'under him' than any other person in town!

Rest in Peace

Some tombstone inscriptions could easily be misunderstood. One read:

> William Jones, beloved Husband of Elizabeth Jones
> Rest in peace until I come.

Another read:

> Erected to the Memory
> of
> John McFarlane
> Drown'd in the Water of Leith
> By a few affectionate friends.

A tombstone in Dorchester Abbey records the miserliness of the deceased.

> Here lies one who for medicine would not give
> A little gold, and so his life was lost;
> I fancy that he'd wish again to live,
> Did he but know how much his funeral cost.

Another bore the not very complimentary inscription:

> Beneath this silent stone is laid,
> A noisy antiquated maid.
> Who from the cradle talked till death
> And ne'er before was out of breath.

Robert Benchley the American humorist once attended a Hollywood party. Each guest was asked to compose their own epitaph. Sitting next to him was an actress whose love affairs and broken marriages were notorious. When she requested his help, he suggested, 'At last she sleeps alone.'

There is a famous tombstone in Wales which has the following inscription:

'Here in 1756 was buried the leg and thigh of Henry Hughes. With the remainder of his body he set off to America to Make his fame and fortune.'

Though he had literally one foot in the grave, he put his best foot forward!

In a Peanuts cartoon, Linus is throwing a stick for Snoopy to retrieve. His first dog-instinct is just to do what is expected of him, chase the stick. But Snoopy finally decides against doing this. 'After I am gone,' he says, 'I want people to have more to say about me than just, "He was a nice guy. He chased sticks."' A development in the American funeral business – talking tombstones – now allows you to have a tombstone that will tell the world about you. Naturally you have to record the message before you die! The playback mechanism is powered by solar energy, and activated by a button, which interested passers-by can press. Though I have grave reservations about such talking tombstones they do raise the question as to what we would choose out of our lives as worth remembering? Some very wise things have been written on tombstones. My own favourites include the epitaphs which Benjamin Franklin and Ben Travers suggested for their own tombstones:

The body of Benjamin Franklin, printer
(Like the cover of an old book,
Its contents worn out,
And stript of its lettering and gilding)
Lies here, food for worms!
Yet the work itself shall not be lost,
For it will, as he believed, appear once more
In a new and beautiful edition,
Corrected and amended
By its author!

Ben Travers, who died at the age of ninety-five, was the author of many humorous plays which were performed in the 1930s and 40s. In his autobiography he described himself as a confirmed Christian. He had no desire to have a tombstone erected in his honour, but insisted if one was to be erected, it should have engraved on it the words, 'This is where the real fun begins.'

Some people have suggested humorous epitaphs for their tombstones:

'Here lies a man whose ideals were so high that he never tried to realise them.'

'Here is something I want to get off my chest.'

'I told you I was sick.'

A Connecticut dentist requested:

'When on this tomb you gaze with gravity
Cheer up! I'm filling my last cavity.'

Jim Watt the former Scottish world boxing champion suggested that they might write on his tombstone:

'Count as long as you like – I'm not getting up this time.'

Other suggestions for tombstones have been:

'This is all over my head.'

'This one is on me.'

Exit Laughing

A lady sitting next to a witty bishop at dinner observed in the course of the conversation, 'My aunt was prevented at the last moment from sailing on the *Titanic*. Would you call that the intervention of Providence?' 'I'm sorry, I can't tell,' replied the bishop. 'I didn't know your aunt.'

&

A Lewis farmer and his wife had three distinguished sons. One was a surgeon, one was a professor and the other an eminent lawyer. When a neighbour noticed them all working on their father's farm, digging a drain, he inquired, 'Is this the brain drain?'

&

Why pay money to have your family tree traced. Go into politics and your opponents will do it for you.

&

The Rev James Dow, recalling the ill-effects of an early pipe and cigar smoking session, said, 'I would offer this advice to any boy who is thinking of taking up smoking. Remember that after Old King Cole sent for his pipe, he sent for his bowl.'

&

When the mother of a student at Jesus College Oxford was asked by a friend for news of her son, she said, 'He's been at Christ's Hospital for some years, but now he has gone up to Jesus.' 'Oh, the poor mite,' said her friend.

&

Mary was a town girl. She knew almost nothing about farm life until she married a man who farmed in the Carse of Gowrie. She found the adjustments involved quite traumatic. She began married life well, getting up with her husband at six o'clock, but within a few weeks he was seeing himself out. One bitterly cold winter's day he returned to the farm around nine for his breakfast. Finding the ashes still in the grate, and his wife still in bed, he called from the foot of the stairs, 'Fire. Fire.' Rushing out of the bedroom, she cried, 'Where, John?' 'In every other farm in the Carse of Gowrie!' he replied.

🦂

I love the story of the Clydebank woman who was extracted from the rubble of her house during the 1940 air raids. When asked by her rescuers where her husband was, she replied, 'The coward is away fighting in North Africa.'

🦂

A bachelor bishop of the Episcopal Church in America, William Cannon, tells how, when his friends were keen that he should stand for bishop, they told him his chances of being elected would be enhanced if he was to find a wife. 'But,' he said, 'I told them. What will I do with her if I am elected?'

🦂

When a wife phoned her husband at work to tell him that the car had water in the carburettor, he graciously said, 'Don't worry dear. Where is the car? I'll get a mechanic to come out.' 'Unfortunately,' she replied, 'It's in the river.'

🦂

In a trembling voice a worried young wife said to the butcher, 'Please give me something that doesn't burn.'

🦂

A Scottish farmer's wife was the kind of woman who had enough mouth for two sets of teeth. From early morning until night, everyone on the farm, especially her husband, was subjected to her perpetual tongue-lash. One night Tom, one of the farmhands, came to the back door to see if he could borrow the stable lantern. 'Where are you going tonight?' inquired the farmer. 'Courting,' was the reply. 'Courting,' exclaimed the farmer with a twinkle in his eye.

'You don't need a lantern to go courting surely? I never took one when I went courting.' 'I can well believe that,' said Tom with a malicious glint in his eye, 'and look what you got.'

🐒

Noah to his wife. 'Do me a favour. Stop saying, "Into each life some rain must fall".'

🐒

For Sale notice: Complete thirty volumes of *Encyclopedia Britannica*. Latest edition. Never used. My wife knows everything.

🐒

A Mrs Finlay tells how, during their honeymoon, one night she found a large spider in the bath in the hotel. Calling to her husband she said, 'Could you get rid of it. My mother always took them away for me.' Her six-foot-tall husband looked very sheepish. 'So did my mother,' he replied.

🐒

The trouble with New Year resolutions is that your wife remembers the ones you make.

🐒

A woman lunching with friends listened to descriptions of elaborate alarm systems, guard dogs and whatnot, that her friends had turned to as protection against burglars. Asked what steps she had taken, she pointed out that she had five small children. 'If a burglar came into my bedroom in the middle of the night, I would probably get up, take him by the hand and lead him to the bathroom.'

🐒

A man who advertised in the papers for a wife got hundreds of replies. Though they varied slightly, the replies said essentially the same thing: 'Dear sir, with regard to your advert for a wife, you can have mine.'

🐒

One day during the rush hour, a Glasgow bus conductor put his arm firmly down between two women in the bus queue, and said, 'Full up. Next bus please.' The last lady to get on, pointing to the lady behind her, said anxiously, 'But that is my mother.' Turning to the older lady he said, 'All right, one more then. I once separated a mother from her daughter. Never again.'

A lady tells how her mother-in-law always sends an anniversary card, and it always arrives one day early. She also phones on the right day. She finally explained the reason for the early card. 'I know John has a memory like a sieve, but when he sees the card he at least knows he has twenty-four hours to buy you a present.

A lady and her husband visited their son in his new flat. When she offered to make a cup of tea, she discovered all the cups were filled with sugar. His flat-mate had seen an attractive girl in the lift, and keen to meet her, had borrowed cups of sugar from each house in the apartment block until he tracked her down.

Professor MacRobert, my former Maths Professor at Glasgow University, had an identical twin brother. In his later years he became slightly absent-minded. Aware of this, the Professor's lovely wife warned the new domestic help that if ever her husband did or said anything strange, not to upset him by drawing his attention to it, but instead to come and tell her about it. The home-help had only been there a week when the door bell rang. There at the door was Professor MacRobert's identical twin brother. Not knowing that this brother existed, she dashed through to Mrs MacRobert in the kitchen and exclaimed, 'Your husband's at the door asking if he's in!'